Mystery of the Two Covenants

Becoming the Bride of Christ, Volume 1

Leo Gaviao

Published by Leo Gaviao, 2024.

MYSTERY OF THE TWO COVENANTS

First edition. December 16, 2024.

ISBN: 979-8230170426

Written by Leo Gaviao.

In sacred scrolls, the promise lies, A Bride redeemed beneath the skies. Through wilderness, her steps are led, By blood and love, the price was paid.

The old fulfilled, the new begun, A Bride prepared for the Risen One. Covenant sealed, the feast draws near, The voice of the Bridegroom calls: "I'm here."

In sacred scrolls, the promise lies, A Bride redeemed beneath the skies. Through wilderness, her steps are led, By blood and love, the price was paid.

The old fulfilled, the new begun, A Bride prepared for the Risen One. Covenant sealed, the feast draws near, The voice of the Bridegroom calls: "I'm here."

Contents

MYSTERY OF THE TWO COVENANTS

This book will help you understand how you become Christ's bride and the covenantal relationship you have in Christ as His bride. The well-researched expose of the nature of covenants in the Old Testament will give you a fresh insight and understanding of the covenant you are in with Christ.

Isaac Migioni (Pastor Kings Bible Church, Bulawayo)

Thoroughly enjoyed reading the book. It is well and passionately written, the author demonstrates a deep and profound understanding of the subject matter.

Bianca Stevens

This is really good, a really good book

I can't believe that he wrote this!

Ps. Moses Chipapa (Movement Church, Harare)

This book is a critical read for understanding the differences between the Old and New Covenants in the Bible. It explains how to live a purely New Covenant life as a follower of Christ. Gaviao covers the nature of God as a God of covenants, the two covenants, and the transition from one to the other. He also explains the meaning and impact of true New Covenant living in various areas of Christian experience.Without this knowledge, believers will struggle against sin, self, defeat, and discouragement. Totally essential for understanding the

LEO GAVIAO

Kingdom of God and the Church's role in it.
Reverend Gift Tryson Kaira (CCAP, Johannesburg)

Preface

The disconnect between the Old and New Testaments has long puzzled believers. Why do the Son of God's teachings seem to contradict His Father's law? This dilemma has troubled many, including longtime Christians.

"Mystery of the Two Covenants" tackles this issue head-on, exploring the biblical concept of covenant to uncover the unity underlying these sacred covenants between God and humanity.

As a disciple of Jesus, I've often wondered how the Old Testament's emphasis on law and obedience relates to Jesus' message of grace and love. This book is the culmination of my journey to understand the connection between the Old and New Testaments.

Through a deep dive into scripture, the covenants within, and extra-biblical research, I believe I've found the answer. Everything hinges on covenant! It has now become my mission to help other believers uncover this truth.

In this book, we'll explore the covenantal nature of the Old and New Testaments, examining how God's plan of redemption unfolds. My prayer is that, together, we'll discover the unity and beauty of God's redemptive plan.

Delbert R. Hillers, in "The Biblical Concept of Covenant," notes that the Hebrew term for "covenant" (berith) encompasses various meanings, including treaty, contract, and marriage (Hillers, 38). This nuanced understanding of covenant is essential for grasping the relationship between the Testaments.

As we delve into the complex covenantal nature of the Old and New Testaments, I pray that you'll gain a deeper understanding of God's plan of redemption, just as I have.

Chapter 1: Behold, I Do a New Thing!

Luke 3:7-17 marks a transformative moment in the biblical narrative, as John the Baptist's preaching sets the stage for a revolutionary shift in God's relationship with humanity. As a Jewish itinerant prophet, John's message resonated with the Israelites, but it also challenged their understanding of God's covenant.

"He said therefore to the crowds that came out to be baptized by him, "You brood of vipers! Who warned you to flee from the wrath to come?

Bear fruits in keeping with repentance. And do not begin to say to yourselves, 'We have Abraham as our father.' For I tell you, God is able from these stones to raise up children for Abraham."

(Luke 3:7-8)

John's message was not merely a call to individual repentance but also a critique of the Jewish establishment. The late David Flusser, professor of Early Christianity and Judaism of the Second Temple Period at the Hebrew University of Jerusalem, observes that John's preaching was characterized by intense earnestness and gravity, shaking the very foundations of Israel's spiritual complacency. His preaching was characterized by "intense earnestness and solemnity, which echoed Isaiah's prophecy:

"Remember not the former things, nor consider the things of old. Behold, I am doing a new thing: now it springs forth, do you not perceive it? I will make a way in the wilderness and rivers in the desert." (Isaiah 43:18-19)

John the Baptist's message underscores a pivotal moment in the biblical narrative and even though it resonated with the Israelites, it challenged their understanding of God's covenant.

John's voice thundered out a warning, urgent and insistent: *""You brood of vipers, who warned you to flee from the wrath [of God that is] to come? Therefore, produce fruit that is worthy of [and consistent with your] repentance [that is, live changed lives, turn from sin and seek God and His righteousness]." (Luke 3:7-8)".*

This metaphor, "brood of vipers," was also adopted by Jesus when he addressed the Pharisees in Matthew 12:34 and was designed to shock the establishment with the hope that they would check themselves and perhaps repent.

John even declared, "God is able to raise up children for Abraham from these stones" (Luke 3:8), challenging the notion that biological descent from Abraham guarantees salvation.

When the crowd asked John what they should do, he didn't simply point them back to the Law. Instead, he emphasized the need for genuine transformation, urging them to produce "fruit worthy of repentance"

"Whoever has two tunics is to share with him who has none, and whoever has food is to do likewise."

Tax collectors also came to be baptized and said to him, "Teacher, what shall we do?"

And he said to them, "Collect no more than you are authorized to do."

Soldiers also asked him, "And we, what shall we do?" And he said to them, "Do not extort money from anyone by threats or by false accusation, and be content with your wages."

MYSTERY OF THE TWO COVENANTS

As the people were in expectation, and all were questioning in their hearts concerning John, whether he might be the Christ, John answered them all, saying, "I baptize you with water, but he who is mightier than I is coming, the strap of whose sandals I am not worthy to untie. He will baptize you with the Holy Spirit and fire.

His winnowing fork is in his hand, to clear his threshing floor and to gather the wheat into his barn, but the chaff he will burn with unquenchable fire." (Luke 3:11-17)

Notably, John also questioned the crowd's claim to be Abraham's descendants, despite their meticulous observance of the Mosaic Law. This challenge highlights the complex relationship between Abraham's promise and the Mosaic Law, suggesting that being a true descendant of Abraham requires more than just outward obedience.

George E. Mendenhall, in "The Covenant Concept," highlights a crucial distinction between the Abrahamic and Mosaic covenants (Mendenhall, 152). The Abrahamic covenant emphasizes God's promise and faith, whereas the Mosaic covenant focuses on law and obedience. This distinction underscores the tension between the two covenants.

In effect John's preaching heralded the advent of a new dispensation and his declaration of the advent of the Messiah bore testimony to that fact.:

"John answered them all by saying, I baptize you with water; but He Who is mightier than I is coming, the strap of Whose sandals I am not fit to unfasten. He will baptize you with the Holy Spirit and with fire." (Luke 3:16).

Whereas in the Levitical era baptism by immersion in water was the ultimate declaration of repentance this new era is characterized by the Messiah's baptism with the Holy Spirit and fire.

Isaiah 43:18-19 provides a prophetic backdrop for John's message:

"Remember not the former things, nor consider the things of old. Behold, I am doing a new thing; now it springs forth, do you not perceive it? I will make a way in the wilderness and rivers in the desert."

This passage prophesies a new era of God's relationship with Israel, marking a significant shift from the old covenant. Delbert R. Hillers notes that the Hebrew term for "remember" (zakar) can also mean "to turn away from" or "cease to observe" (Hillers, 44). This interpretation supports the idea that John's message marks a significant shift in God's relationship with Israel.

John the Baptist's preaching marked the culmination of the old covenant era and its associated priesthood, while ushering in a new era characterized by a new covenant, a new kind of priesthood, and a distinctively different law. This new dispensation prioritizes faith, repentance, and transformation, heralding a profound shift from the Mosaic Law. As we unravel the Mystery of the Two Testaments, we'll delve deeper into the far-reaching implications of this new covenant, exploring how it redefines our understanding of God's relationship with humanity.

References:

- Edersheim, A. (1883). The Life and Times of Jesus the Messiah. New York: Longmans, Green, and Co.

- Flusser, D. (1965). The Judaism of the Second Temple Period. Jerusalem: Magnes Press.

- Mendenhall, G. E. (1954). The Covenant Concept in the Bible. Journal of Biblical Literature, 73(3), 151-162.

- Hillers, D. R. (1969). The Biblical Concept of Covenant. Journal of Theological Studies, 20(1), 37-48.

Chapter 2: Abraham, the Father of Those Being Saved

Introduction

It is an undeniable truth that the old must yield to the new, yet paradoxically, embracing the new often necessitates a profound understanding of the old.

Likewise, for us to have a full appreciation of the New Covenant that Jesus offers us we must understand the Old Covenant. This retrospective gaze allows us to appreciate the surpassing excellence of this New Covenant over its antecedent.

Regrettably, I have come to realize that many of us have never truly grasped the underlying essence of the Old Testament covenants, which in turn has hindered our comprehension of the covenant that Jesus inaugurated. By neglecting to understand the foundational covenantal framework of the Old Testament, we inadvertently diminish our appreciation for the transformative power and redemptive significance of the New Covenant.

"Upon closer examination, the Pentateuch, commonly referred to as the first five books of the Bible, reveals itself to be a compilation of distinct covenants between God, Abraham, and his descendants.

In my opinion, it would be more accurate to designate this collection as the Old Covenant. The term 'Testament' connotes a testimony, memorandum, or record. Consequently, the books of the Pentateuch in the Old Testament can be viewed as a transcription of the memorandum or record of the old covenants between God and the Jewish nation. This raises an intriguing question: why did God establish multiple covenants, rather than a single, all-encompassing one? What was the underlying purpose of these covenants, and what did they entail?"

Notably, research by G.E. Mendenhall reveals that ancient Hebraic covenants were fundamentally relational in nature, rather than merely contractual agreements. This distinction is beautifully illustrated in the life of Abraham, whose profound relationship with God embodies the very essence of these relational covenants

The Jewish nation is first identified in the biblical narrative during the time of Abraham (Genesis 11:27). Abraham, initially known as Abram, enjoyed a remarkably intimate relationship with God, as evident in the poignant encounter described in Genesis 18:1-2. In this passage, Abraham's spiritual sensitivity is highlighted as he recognizes God from afar, despite His appearance in human form

"And the LORD appeared to him by the oaks of Mamre, as he sat at the door of his tent in the heat of the day. He lifted up his eyes and looked, and behold, three men were standing in front of him. When he saw them, he ran from the tent door to meet them and bowed himself to the earth." (Gen 18:1-2)

Abraham had cultivated the art of serving and waiting upon the Lord, and remarkably, God delighted in accepting his service. As Abraham himself humbly expressed, 'If I have found favor in thy sight' (Genesis 18:3), he had indeed gained a profound level of favor with God, to the extent that God was pleased to receive his acts of service and worship.

"...and said, my lord, if now I have found favor in your sight, do not pass by your servant, I beg of you.
Let a little water be brought, and you may wash your feet and recline and rest yourselves under the tree.
And I will bring a morsel (mouthful) of bread to refresh and sustain your hearts before you go on further—for that is why you have come to your servant. And they replied, do as you have said.
So Abraham hastened into the tent to Sarah and said, Quickly, get ready three measures of fine meal, knead it, and bake cakes.
And Abraham ran to the herd and brought a calf tender and good and gave it to the young man [to butcher]; then he [Abraham] hastened to prepare it.
And he took curds and milk and the calf which he had made ready, and set it before [the men]; and he stood by them under the tree while they ate."
(Gen18:3-8)

Abraham's life is a remarkable testament to the power of finding favor in the eyes of the Lord. What's striking is that he lived in an era before the giving of the Law, which implies that his righteous standing before God wasn't based on his adherence to a set of rules or regulations. And yet, God chose to honor him in a profoundly personal way, paying him a visit and sharing a meal at his table – a truly extraordinary display of favor and intimacy. But what lies at the heart of this extraordinary relationship? What was it about Abraham that prompted God to bestow upon him such unprecedented favor and intimacy?"

Faith, Humility, and Obedience

NOW [in Haran] the Lord said to Abram, go for yourself [for your own advantage] away from your country, from your relatives and your father's house, to the land that I will show you. And I will make of you a great nation, and I will bless you [with abundant increase of favors] and make your name famous and distinguished, and you will be a blessing [dispensing good to others].

And I will bless those who bless you [who confer prosperity or happiness upon you] and curse him who curses or uses insolent language toward you; in you will all the families and kindred of the earth be blessed [and by you they will bless themselves].
So Abram departed, as the Lord had directed him; and Lot [his nephew] went with him. Abram was seventy-five years old when he left Haran.
(Gen 12:1-4)

Abraham's response to God's call in Genesis 12:1-4 is a shining example of his unwavering faith, profound humility, and unreserved obedience. As the book of Hebrews so eloquently attests, Abraham's remarkable journey of trust and surrender serves as a timeless paradigm of what it means to walk by faith

And without faith it is impossible to please him, for whoever would draw near to God must believe that he exists and that he rewards those who seek him.

By faith Noah, being warned by God concerning events as yet unseen, in reverent fear constructed an ark for the saving of his household. By this he condemned the world and became an heir of the righteousness that comes by faith.

MYSTERY OF THE TWO COVENANTS

By faith Abraham obeyed when he was called to go out to a place that he was to receive as an inheritance. And he went out, not knowing where he was going.
By faith he went to live in the land of promise, as in a foreign land, living in tents with Isaac and Jacob, heirs with him of the same promise.
For he was looking forward to the city that has foundations, whose designer and builder is God. (Heb. 11:6-10)

Abraham heard, believed and obeyed God!

The foundation of obedience is humility, which, in turn, is grounded in two essential pillars: trust and faith. Trust that the one who gives the command possesses wisdom and knowledge, and faith that the instructions provided will yield the desired results when followed. This synergy of trust, faith, and humility empowers individuals to surrender their will and obey with confidence and assurance.

In the biblical narrative, Abraham's relationship with God exemplifies this dynamic, built as it was on faith, humility, and obedience. His humility was rooted in trust and faith in God's character and ability. In the cultural context of the ancient Near East, their covenantal relationship was forged through a solemn and binding agreement, often carrying severe consequences for breach (Mendenhall, 1954). By entering into this covenant, God established trust through a revered and culturally recognized institution.

This covenantal framework provided a foundation for trust and cooperation. Humility is evident in the willingness to heed God's command, demonstrating trust in God's benevolent character and assurance that God has the individual's best interests at heart. This humility stems from trust in God's ability to fulfill His promises, as outlined in the covenant's stipulations and sanctions (Hillers, 1969). The ritual and sacrificial elements of the covenant reinforced faith and obedience, underscoring the gravity and solemnity of the agreement.

Ultimately, this relationship embodies three qualities that God highly esteems: faith, humility, and obedience. Notably, faith is not blind, but rather rooted in God's demonstrated character and ability, as evident in the covenant's historical prologue (Genesis 15:1-21). This covenantal framework provides unwavering assurance of God's commitment, fostering an environment of trust, cooperation, and mutual understanding.

By honoring the covenant, Abraham acknowledged the consequences of breach, including divine sanctions and curses (Kline, 1972). Conversely, his obedience opened the door to covenantal blessings, solidifying his relationship with God.

The Dynamics of God and Abraham's Covenant Relationship

The relationship between Abraham and God shares parallels with the marital bond, founded on the essential pillars of faith, humility, and obedience. This dynamic is pivotal in understanding biblical covenants, which were a common feature of ancient Near Eastern culture (Wenham, "The Bible Speaks Today: Genesis 1-15," 244). By establishing a covenant with Abraham, God utilized a culturally recognized institution to foster trust and deepen their relationship.

Abraham's faith was exemplified when, at 75, he believed God's promise to make him the father of a nation (Genesis 12:1-3, 15:5-6). This faith was rooted in his trust in God's sovereignty, despite humanly impossible circumstances (Romans 4:19-21). Abraham's faith was characterized by a servant's heart, marked by a willingness to surrender personal plans and desires to God's will, reliance on God's guidance, submission to God's authority, selfless obedience, and availability to follow God's lead.

Abraham's humility was evident in his willingness to follow God's instructions without question, exemplifying a servant's heart that prioritizes God's will, trusts God's sovereignty, and serves others. This faith, humility, and servant's heart inspired obedience, allowing God to guide Abraham's destiny.

Similarly, when Eleazar sought a wife for Isaac, he looked for a woman with a servant's heart (Genesis 24:13-14), a quality essential in covenant relationships where faith, humility, and obedience are vital.

Abraham's friendship with God, as described in Isaiah 41:8, was a unique and intimate bond modeled after the covenant relationship. The Hebrew word for "friend" (אָהֵב, 'âhab) conveys deep affection, highlighting the profound nature of their connection.

In Genesis 18:17-19, God declares,

"For I know him, that he will command his children and his household after him, and they shall keep the way of the LORD." The Hebrew word "know" (יָדַע, yâda') implies an intimate and experiential knowledge, akin to the familiarity between a husband and wife (Genesis 4:1).

The intimacy between Abraham and God is essential to understanding their covenant relationship. A notable example of this depth is Abraham's intercession for Sodom and Gomorrah (Genesis 18:22-33). Significantly, God shared His plans with Abraham primarily as a natural extension of their covenant friendship, with Abraham's successful intercession for Lot and his family being a secondary outcome. This decision to confide in Abraham demonstrates the trust and familiarity inherent in their covenantal bond.

In the context of ancient Hebraic covenants, parties were committed to mutual obligations, with consequences for breach. God's covenant with Abraham established a framework for their relationship, marked by faithfulness, trust, and obedience. This covenantal foundation fostered a profound and enduring connection between Abraham and God.

The Nature of Biblical Friendship

The biblical concept of friendship surpasses modern understanding (Deuteronomy 13:6, Proverbs 17:17, 18:24). Biblical friendship encompasses five key elements:

1. Covenant commitment: A deep, binding relationship (1 Samuel 18:1-4, 20:42)

2. Mutual loyalty: Unwavering support and faithfulness (Ruth 1:16-17, 2 Samuel 15:21)

3. Emotional intimacy: Sharing joys, sorrows, and deepest thoughts (2 Samuel 1:26, Psalm 55:13-14)

4. Spiritual accountability: Encouraging growth, confronting sin (Proverbs 27:5-6, Galatians 6:1-2)

5. Selfless love: Putting the other's interests above one's own (John 15:13, Romans 5:8)

Abraham's friendship with God exemplified these qualities, demonstrating a deep, covenantal relationship. God sought a worthy friend in Abraham, through whom He could fulfill His desire for a family. To appreciate the evolution of God and Abraham's relationship, understanding ancient Hebraic covenants is crucial. This knowledge illuminates Abraham's interactions with God, distinctly marked by covenants.

Conclusion

The concept of covenant relationship, that we see in God's pact with Abraham, presents a paradigm for understanding the divine-human dynamic. This relationship, rooted in faith, humility, and obedience, is reminiscent of the sacred bond between a husband and wife. The Hebrew term for "covenant" (בְּרִית, bərît) implies a deep, binding commitment, underscoring the intimacy and mutual obligations inherent in this relationship.

In the context of ancient Hebraic covenants, parties were committed to mutual obligations, with consequences for breach. God's covenant with Abraham established a framework for their relationship, marked by faithfulness, trust, and obedience. This covenantal foundation fostered a profound and enduring connection between Abraham and God, prefiguring the greater covenantal relationship between God the Father and Israel.

The dynamics of God's relationship with Abraham are remarkably similar to those of a human marriage. God initiates the covenant, just as a husband would initiate a marriage proposal. Abraham responds with faith and obedience, just as a wife would pledge her loyalty and commitment to her husband. Throughout their relationship, God and Abraham engage in a dialogue of mutual love, trust, and submission, echoing the intimacy and vulnerability characteristic of a healthy marital relationship.

This parallel between God's covenant with Abraham and human marriage is not coincidental. The biblical authors deliberately employed marital imagery to convey the depth and intimacy of God's relationship with His people. By doing so, they highlighted the covenantal nature of this relationship, emphasizing the mutual obligations, responsibilities, and commitments that undergird it.

In the Old Testament, the prophet Isaiah employs marital imagery to describe God's relationship with Israel, declaring, "For your Maker is your husband, the Lord of hosts is his name" (Isaiah 54:5). Similarly, the prophet Hosea depicts God as a husband who loves, redeems, and restores His bride, Israel (Hosea 2:16-20). These marital metaphors underscore the intimacy, loyalty, and commitment that characterize God's covenant relationship with His people.

As we reflect on the significance of God's covenant with Abraham, we are reminded that our relationship with God is not merely a contractual agreement; it is a deeply personal and intimate bond. We are invited to participate in a divine marriage contract, one that is marked by faithfulness, trust, and obedience. As we respond to this invitation, we embark on a journey of mutual love, trust, and submission, echoing the intimacy and vulnerability characteristic of a healthy marital relationship.

References:

(Mendenhall, 1954) Mendenhall, G. E. Covenant Forms in Israelite Tradition. Journal of Biblical Literature, 73(3), 195-204.

(Hillers, 1969) Hillers, D. R. Covenant: The History of a Biblical Concept.

(Kline, 1972) Kline, M. G. The Structure of Biblical Authority.

- Mendenhall, G. E. (1954). The Covenant Concept in the Bible. Journal of Biblical Literature, 73(3), 151-162.

- Wenham, G. J. (1987). The Bible Speaks Today: Genesis 1-15. Leicester: Inter-Varsity Press.

Chapter 3: Biblical Covenant

The Significance of Covenant

The pivotal role of covenant in God's interactions with humanity is a recurring theme throughout biblical history. Whenever God initiates a significant move that profoundly impacts humanity's destiny, He consistently employs covenant as the mechanism for connection. This pattern underscores the centrality of covenant in God's relational dynamic with humanity.

The establishment of covenants is a deliberate act on God's part, driven by His desire to establish, restore, or redefine His relationship with mankind. Whether it is the Adamic Covenant, the Noahic Covenant, the Abrahamic Covenant, the Mosaic Covenant, or the Davidic Covenant, each covenantal agreement serves as a vital instrument in bridging the chasm between God's divine nature and humanity's frailty.

This restorative function of covenant is rooted in God's character as a faithful, loving, and merciful God. As sin entered the world, humanity's relationship with God was severely fractured. However, through the establishment of covenants, God provided a mechanism for restoring this relationship. By establishing clear terms, responsibilities, and promises, covenants facilitate a deep, binding commitment between God and humanity.

The Hebrew concept of covenant (בְּרִית, bərîṯ) implies a mutually binding agreement, marked by faithfulness, trust, and obedience. This covenantal framework is rooted in the ancient

Hebraic tradition, where covenants were employed to establish relationships, resolve conflicts, and facilitate reconciliation.

In the context of God's covenants with humanity, this relational dynamic is particularly significant. God's covenants are not merely contractual agreements; they represent a deep, binding commitment between God and humanity. This commitment is rooted in God's character, as evidenced by His faithfulness, loving-kindness, and mercy.

The restorative function of covenant is also evident in the person of Jesus Christ. As the ultimate covenantal fulfillment, Jesus embodied the faithful, loving, and merciful character of God. Through His life, death, and resurrection, Jesus established a new covenant, one that would reconcile humanity to God and restore the fractured relationship between God and humanity (Hebrews 8:6-13, 9:15-28).

Understanding Covenant: Essential for Spiritual Clarity

Recognizing the pivotal role of covenant in biblical theology is essential for grasping the intricacies of God's redemptive plan. As George Mendenhall (1954, p. 15) astutely observes, "covenant is the central concept in biblical theology." By delving into the nuances of covenantal dynamics, we gain profound insight into the very fabric of God's interactions with humanity.

Firstly, the covenantal paradigm reveals God's inherently relational nature and His ardent desire for intimacy with humanity. The biblical narrative is replete with examples of God's unwavering longing for connection with His people. From the inaugural covenant with Adam in the Garden of

Eden to the ultimate covenantal fulfillment in Jesus Christ, God's desire for intimacy with humanity is a recurring theme that permeates the entirety of Scripture. Covenant serves as the divinely ordained mechanism for facilitating this intimacy, providing a framework for mutual commitment, loyalty, and obedience.

Secondly, the dynamics of covenant illuminate the underlying principles that govern God's interactions with His people. The Hebrew concept of covenant (בְּרִית, bərîṯ) implies a mutually binding agreement, marked by faithfulness, trust, and obedience. This covenantal framework is rooted in the ancient Hebraic tradition, where covenants were employed to establish relationships, resolve conflicts, and facilitate reconciliation. By examining the intricacies of covenantal principles, we gain profound insight into God's expectations for His people, as well as the consequences of covenantal disobedience.

Thirdly, the covenantal paradigm underscores the paramount importance of faith, obedience, and loyalty in the divine-human dynamic. The biblical narrative is replete with examples of individuals who exemplified these covenantal virtues, such as Abraham, Moses, and David. Conversely, the consequences of covenantal disobedience are also starkly evident, as seen in the examples of Adam, Saul, and Israel's repeated covenantal infidelities. By exploring the covenantal paradigm, we gain a deeper understanding of the principles that govern God's interactions with humanity.

Biblical Examples Illustrating Covenant's Importance

1. God's covenant with Abraham (Genesis 15:1-21): Demonstrates God's commitment to His people and the importance of faith and obedience.

2. The Mosaic Covenant (Exodus 19-24): Establishes Israel's national identity and covenantal responsibilities.

3. The Davidic Covenant (2 Samuel 7:1-17): Illustrates God's promise to establish a royal lineage and eternal kingdom.

Defining Covenant: Covenant: A Relational Framework

Western cultural perspectives often overlook the nuances of the Hebraic covenant paradigm. Our non-Hebraic cultures and mindsets lack a paradigm matching this Hebraic definition. Embracing this paradigm is crucial for becoming what God ordained. Our inclusion in the Body of Christ hinges on joining and becoming part of an organic relational body bound together by covenant. Biblical covenant transcends mere contractual obligations, promises, or agreements. It embodies a dynamic, living relationship between God and His people. This relational essence is rooted in the Hebrew word "Berîyth" (בְּרִית), meaning "to cut." However, its connotations extend far beyond a simple transaction.

The Significance of "Berîyth"

"Berîyth" is intimately connected to "Bârah" (בְּרָה), which encompasses various meanings:

MYSTERY OF THE TWO COVENANTS

1. To select: Implying a deliberate choice, underscoring God's sovereign initiative in establishing covenantal relationships.

2. To feed: Symbolizing mutual nourishment and sustenance within the covenant.

3. To cause to eat: Highlighting the sharing of food and communal celebration.

4. To manifest: Emphasizing the public declaration and recognition of the covenant.

In biblical context, "Berîyth" signifies cutting for the purpose of:

1. Eating together: Sharing a meal, symbolizing unity and fellowship.

2. Sharing food: Demonstrating mutual provision and care.

3. Preparing a banquet: Celebrating the initiation of an ongoing relationship

Examples of the relational nature of biblical covenants can be found when we study Abraham's Covenant (Genesis 15:1-21): in which God's covenantal promise is sealed through a sacrificial meal, emphasizing their relational bond. In the Mosaic Covenant (Exodus 24:1-11) Israel's covenant with God was also ratified through a communal meal, signifying their collective commitment. We will also learn that the New Covenant (Luke 22:7-20) was instituted via the last supper during which Jesus shared a meal with his disciples.

The relational nature of covenants is distinguished by three indispensable components. Firstly, covenants entail mutual commitment, which involves active engagement, loyalty, and a deep sense of responsibility towards one another. Secondly, shared responsibilities are a hallmark of covenantal relationships, ensuring that all parties share both the obligations and benefits inherent in the agreement. Finally, relational intimacy is a vital aspect of covenantal dynamics, fostering a profound connection and communion with God that nurtures a deeply personal and transformative relationship.

As we learnt in the previous chapter, Abraham's covenant relationship with God exemplifies the dynamics of a divine marriage contract – the ketubah (marriage contract).

The Ketubah – and ancient Hebraic Legal Instrument

The ketubah, an ancient Hebraic legal instrument, plays a significant role in Jewish tradition and to some extent has been on the periphery of biblical studies. This marriage contract, rooted in faith, humility, and obedience, represents a binding agreement between two parties, outlining the terms, responsibilities, and expectations of their relationship. While the ketubah has historically not been a central concept in biblical theology per se even though its study can inform our understanding of biblical covenantal relationships and the Jewish context in which they emerged.

In the Hebrew context, covenants are a pervasive theme, and the ketubah serves as a notable example of a recorded covenantal marriage agreement. Interestingly, the traditional ketubah often incorporates elements of four ancient covenants – the Blood/Servanthood covenant, the Salt/Friendship covenant, the Sandal/Sonship covenant, and the Covenant of Praise. These four covenants, woven together in the ketubah, beautifully illustrate the complexity and richness of God's relationships with His people, revealing a multifaceted and deeply personal divine-human dynamic.

Beyond its legal significance, the ketubah also serves as a treasured family heirloom, documenting the personal stories and histories of the couple. Typically, a ketubah would include the family history of the groom, the family history of the bride, as well as the story of how the couple met, providing a poignant and personal touch to the covenantal agreement.

The Blood/Servanthood Covenant

The Blood/Servanthood Covenant is a foundational aspect of the ketubah. This covenant is a relationship into which people entered in to fulfill certain promises to each other. Similar to modern-day contracts, the Blood/Servanthood Covenant established obligations between parties, but unlike modern contracts, these obligations did not expire and could only be nullified upon the death of one or all parties. This covenant served as the basic building block of all covenant relationships, and parties often entered into additional covenants that ran concurrently with this covenant. Notably, the terms of a covenant could not be modified by entering into another covenant; once a covenant was established, it was binding for life. This aspect of covenant reflects the immutable nature and integrity of God.

The traditional blood covenant, a sacred and binding agreement, consisted of nine distinct steps. These steps were deeply rooted in ancient Eastern and Hebraic culture, and each held profound significance.

1. Exchange of Coats or Robes: The two individuals would exchange their coats or robes, symbolizing the exchange of themselves, their lives, and their identities.

2. Exchange of Belts: The parties would remove their belts, which held their swords and other fighting instruments, and offer them to each other. This gesture signified the pledge of protection and loyalty.

3. Cutting the Covenant: An animal would be killed and cut in half, with the two halves laid opposite each other. The two parties would then pass between the halves, invoking a divine curse upon themselves if they were to break the covenant.

4. Mingling of Blood: The parties would cut the palm of their right hand, clasp each other's hand, and mingle their blood. This act symbolized the union of their lives and the intermingling of their very being.

5. Exchange of Names: Each party would take part of the other's name and incorporate it into their own, signifying their newfound identity and unity.

6. Marking with a Scar: A scar or identifying mark would be made on the body, serving as a visible reminder of the covenant and warning others of the consequences of violating it.

7. Declaration of Terms: The parties would stand before a witness and declare the terms of the covenant, including the exchange of assets and liabilities.

8. Memorial Meal: A loaf of bread would be broken in half, and each party would feed the other half to the other, symbolizing the exchange of their bodies and lives. Wine would also be shared, representing the exchange of their blood.

9. Planting a Memorial Tree: A tree would be planted as a memorial to the covenant, and its roots would be sprinkled with the blood of the sacrificed animal. This tree served as a lasting testament to the covenant and its enduring nature.

These nine steps, while not necessarily occurring in this exact order, formed the foundation of the blood covenant. This sacred agreement was entered into with no expiration date in sight, and subsequent covenants built upon previous ones, creating a rich tapestry of relationships and obligations. Ultimately, the blood covenant served as a powerful symbol of the parties' commitment to one another, with the implicit understanding that violating the covenant would incur severe consequences.

The Salt/Friendship Covenant

Entering into a Covenant of Salt signifies an unwavering commitment to loyalty and truthfulness, even unto death. This solemn bond was never undertaken lightly, and it demands profound respect. To the ancient Hebrews, salt embodied purification and symbolized enduring friendship, honesty, and loyalty.

In ancient times, people would often carry small pouches of salt on their belts. When they formed a new friendship during their travels, they would seal their bond with salt. Both parties would take a pinch of salt, combine it in a bowl, and then break bread, dipping it into the shared salt. This act would solemnly seal their covenant.

Next, they would pour half of the intertwined salt back into their respective pouches, forever entwining their lives. Their salt, now inextricably linked, served as a tangible representation of their unbreakable covenant. The only way to dissolve the covenant would be for one party to retrieve their original salt from the other's pouch, an impossible feat.

To further solidify their commitment, the parties would exchange their coats and belts. The coat represented an individual's wealth, while the belt, which carried the sword, symbolized their military strength. By exchanging these items, each party declared their willingness to commit their wealth and strength to the other, essentially saying, "My wealth is yours, and I will die protecting you with my sword."

There are four references for the salt covenant in the Old Testament:

And Melchizedek king of Salem brought out bread and wine. (He was a priest of God Most High.) And he blessed him and said, "Blessed be Abraham by God Most High, Possessor of heaven and earth; and blessed be God Most High, who has delivered your enemies into your hand!" And Abraham gave him a tenth of everything. (Gen 14-18-20)

And Abijah stood up upon mount Zemaraim, which is in mount Ephraim, and said, "Hear me, thou Jeroboam, and all Israel; Ought ye not to know that the LORD God of Israel gave the kingdom over Israel to David forever, even to him and to his sons by a covenant of salt?" (2Ch 13:4-5)

"All the heave offerings of the holy things, which the children of Israel offer unto the LORD, have I given thee, and thy sons and thy daughters with thee, by a statute forever: it is a covenant of salt forever before the LORD unto thee and to thy seed with thee. (Num 18:19)

And every oblation of thy meat (grain) offering shalt thou season with salt; neither shalt thou suffer the salt of the covenant of thy

God to be lacking from thy meat offering: with all thine offerings thou shalt offer salt. (Lev 2:13)

However, I believe that there is an instance where the salt covenant features in the New Testament as well. But let's leave that for a later juncture.

The Sandal/Sonship Covenant

Although the ritual of the sandal covenant is also well established in scripture, not even once does the phrase "sandal covenant" appear in the scriptures.

In ancient Hebrew times, property boundaries were marked out by the owner by walking around the perimeter of his property and boundary markers were often established by inserting old sandals into a group of rocks. These markers were an indication that the land was under the dominion of someone since when one stood on top of someone or something one had dominion over him or it.

A good example of this mindset is given to us in the book of Joshua chapter 10. When the Bible describes to us how Joshua treated the five defeated Amorite Kings that hid in a cave in Makkedah.

Then Joshua said, "Open the mouth of the cave and bring those five kings out to me from the cave." And they did so and brought those five kings out to him from the cave, the king of Jerusalem, the king of Hebron, the king of Jarmuth, the king of Lachish, and the king of Eglon. And when they brought those kings out to Joshua, Joshua summoned all the men of Israel and said to the chiefs of the men of war who had gone with him, "Come near; put your feet on the necks of these kings."

Then they came near and put their feet on their necks. (Jos 10:22-24)

Since the sandal denoted dominion or undisputed ownership the sandal covenant is a relationship entered into when property rights are exchanged or in the case of an inheritance when an heir is given authority over an inheritance to the extent that they have as much power and authority over that inheritance as the one that confers it upon them. This was the case with Joseph in Egypt when Pharoah elevated him and put his signet ring upon his finger. In Hebrew culture when a man child came of age, typically 30 years old, if the father was happy with his sons conduct and confident in his stewardship abilities he would go to the gates of the city and gather at least ten elders then he would declare; "Today, this my child has come of age, I am pleased with him and I adopt him as my son (heir)".

An example of this protocol in action is when Boaz who was Elimelech's family's kinsman redeemer redemeemed his inheritance and married Ruth.

Now Boaz had gone up to the gate and sat down there. And behold, the redeemer, of whom Boaz had spoken, came by. So Boaz said, "Turn aside, friend; sit down here." And he turned aside and sat down.

And he took ten men of the elders of the city and said, "Sit down here." So they sat down.

Then he said to the redeemer, "Naomi, who has come back from the country of Moab, is selling the parcel of land that belonged to our relative Elimelech.

So I thought I would tell you of it and say, 'Buy it in the presence of those sitting here and in the presence of the elders of my people.'

If you will redeem it, redeem it. But if you will not, tell me, that I may know, for there is no one besides you to redeem it, and I come after you." And he said, "I will redeem it."

Then Boaz said, "The day you buy the field from the hand of Naomi, you also acquire Ruth the Moabite, the widow of the dead, in order to perpetuate the name of the dead in his inheritance."

Then the redeemer said, "I cannot redeem it for myself, lest I impair my own inheritance. Take my right of redemption yourself, for I cannot redeem it."

Now this was the custom in former times in Israel concerning redeeming and exchanging: to confirm a transaction, the one drew off his sandal and gave it to the other, and this was the manner of attesting in Israel.

So when the redeemer said to Boaz, "Buy it for yourself," he drew off his sandal.

Then Boaz said to the elders and all the people, "You are witnesses this day that I have bought from the hand of Naomi all that belonged to Elimelech and all that belonged to Chilion and to Mahlon.

Also Ruth the Moabite, the widow of Mahlon, I have bought to be my wife, to perpetuate the name of the dead in his inheritance, that the name of the dead may not be cut off from among his brothers and from the gate of his native place. You are witnesses this day."

Then all the people who were at the gate and the elders said, "We are witnesses. May the LORD make the woman, who is coming into your house, like Rachel and Leah, who together built up the house of Israel. May you act worthily in Ephrathah and be renowned in Bethlehem,

(Rth 4:1-11)

The story of Ruth, Naomi, and Boaz illustrates the significance of the sandal covenant in Hebrew law and tradition. Elimelech's inheritance had at least two potential redeemers, with Boaz being second in line. Following custom, Boaz brought the issue of Elimelech's inheritance before the city elders, prompted by Ruth's approach to him, as instructed by Naomi. Ruth's words, "Spread your wings over your servant, for you are a redeemer" (Ruth 3:3-9), indicated Naomi's willingness to allow Elimelech's inheritance to be redeemed by a kinsman.

When the first kinsman redeemer declined the offer due to the obligation to marry Ruth, Boaz stepped in and accepted the responsibility. To formalize the arrangement, Boaz and the first kinsman redeemer commemorated a sandal covenant by exchanging sandals before the elders at the city gate. This act granted Boaz the rights and authority over Elimelech's inheritance, as well as the right to marry Ruth.

The narrative of the sandal covenant, as seen in the book of Ruth, highlights the far-reaching implications of Hebrew law, particularly for the bride. In the event of a Hebrew man's death without an heir, his widow would lose access to his inheritance. To prevent this, the deceased's brothers were obligated to continue their brother's lineage by marrying the widow and siring a son on his behalf. This law, prescribed in Deuteronomy 25:5-10, ensured the sandal covenant was upheld and the family's inheritance and legacy were preserved.

As we see in Deuteronomy 25:5-10, if brothers live together and one of them dies and has no son, his wife shall not be married outside the family to a stranger [an excluded man].

Her husband's brother shall go in to her and take her as his wife and perform the duty of a husband's brother to her. And the firstborn son shall succeed to the name of the dead brother, that his name may not be blotted out of Israel.

Furthermore, if the man does not want to take his brother's wife, then let his brother's wife go up to the gate to the elders, and say, my husband's brother refuses to continue his brother's name in Israel; he will not perform the duty of my husband's brother. Then the elders of his city shall call him and speak to him. And if he stands firm and says, I do not want to take her, then shall his brother's wife come to him in the presence of the elders and pull his shoe off his foot and spit in his face and shall answer, so shall it be done to that man who does not build up his brother's house. And his family shall be called in Israel, The House of Him Whose Shoe Was Loosed

This issue is brought into sharp perspective by the story of Tamar, Judah's widowed daughter in law.

And Judah took a wife for Er his firstborn, and her name was Tamar.

But Er, Judah's firstborn, was wicked in the sight of the LORD, and the LORD put him to death.

Then Judah said to Onan, "Go in to your brother's wife and perform the duty of a brother-in-law to her, and raise up offspring for your brother."

But Onan knew that the offspring would not be his. So whenever he went in to his brother's wife he would waste the semen on the ground, so as not to give offspring to his brother.

And what he did was wicked in the sight of the LORD, and he put him to death also.

Then Judah said to Tamar his daughter-in-law, "Remain a widow in your father's house, till Shelah my son grows up"—for he feared that he would die, like his brothers. So Tamar went and remained in her father's house.

In the course of time the wife of Judah, Shua's daughter, died. When Judah was comforted, he went up to Timnah to his sheepshearers, he and his friend Hirah the Adullamite.

And when Tamar was told, "Your father-in-law is going up to Timnah to shear his sheep,"

she took off her widow's garments and covered herself with a veil, wrapping herself up, and sat at the entrance to Enaim, which is on the road to Timnah. For she saw that Shelah was grown up, and she had not been given to him in marriage.

When Judah saw her, he thought she was a prostitute, for she had covered her face.

He turned to her at the roadside and said, "Come, let me come in to you," for he did not know that she was his daughter-in-law. She said, "What will you give me, that you may come in to me?" He answered, "I will send you a young goat from the flock." And she said, "If you give me a pledge, until you send it—"

He said, "What pledge shall I give you?" She replied, "Your signet and your cord and your staff that is in your hand." So he gave them to her and went in to her, and she conceived by him. Then she arose and went away, and taking off her veil she put on the garments of her widowhood.

When Judah sent the young goat by his friend the Adullamite to take back the pledge from the woman's hand, he did not find her. And he asked the men of the place, "Where is the cult prostitute who was at Enaim at the roadside?" And they said, "No cult prostitute has been here."

MYSTERY OF THE TWO COVENANTS

So he returned to Judah and said, "I have not found her. Also, the men of the place said, 'No cult prostitute has been here.'" And Judah replied, "Let her keep the things as her own, or we shall be laughed at. You see, I sent this young goat, and you did not find her."

About three months later Judah was told, "Tamar your daughter-in-law has been immoral. Moreover, she is pregnant by immorality." And Judah said, "Bring her out, and let her be burned."

As she was being brought out, she sent word to her father-in-law, "By the man to whom these belong, I am pregnant." And she said, "Please identify whose these are, the signet and the cord and the staff."

Then Judah identified them and said, "She is more righteous than I, since I did not give her to my son Shelah." And he did not know her again. (Gen 38:6-26)

Two significant points emerge from this narrative. Firstly, God's displeasure with Onan's reluctance to sire a son on behalf of his brother is evident, as He struck Onan down and killed him. This serves as a stark reminder of the importance of fulfilling familial obligations.

The second, and even more crucial point to note, is Tamar's desperation for an heir. Her willingness to devise a scheme to get pregnant by her father-in-law, Judah, underscores the immense value placed on producing an heir. This act demonstrates the empowering nature of childbirth for women in Hebrew culture, where bearing an heir was paramount.

Hebrew inheritance law was carefully crafted to ensure that the inheritance remained within the family bloodline. A notable example of this is the story of the daughters of

Zelophehad, which illustrates that a man's inheritance could pass to his daughter if he had no son. However, the inheritance could never be directly passed to his widow. Instead, the widow's access to the inheritance was contingent upon having an heir.

Then drew near the daughters of Zelophehad the son of Hepher, son of Gilead, son of Machir, son of Manasseh, from the clans of Manasseh the son of Joseph. The names of his daughters were: Mahlah, Noah, Hoglah, Milcah, and Tirzah.

And they stood before Moses and before Eleazar the priest and before the chiefs and all the congregation, at the entrance of the tent of meeting, saying,

"Our father died in the wilderness. He was not among the company of those who gathered themselves together against the LORD in the company of Korah, but died for his own sin. And he had no sons.

Why should the name of our father be taken away from his clan because he had no son? Give to us a possession among our father's brothers."

Moses brought their case before the LORD.

And the LORD said to Moses,

"The daughters of Zelophehad are right. You shall give them possession of an inheritance among their father's brothers and transfer the inheritance of their father to them.

And you shall speak to the people of Israel, saying, 'If a man dies and has no son, then you shall transfer his inheritance to his daughter.

And if he has no daughter, then you shall give his inheritance to his brothers.

And if he has no brothers, then you shall give his inheritance to his father's brothers.

And if his father has no brothers, then you shall give his inheritance to the nearest kinsman of his clan, and he shall possess it. And it shall be for the people of Israel a statute and rule, as the LORD commanded Moses."' (Num 27:1-11)

Because of this aspect of inheritance law, bearing an heir was a very important blessing for a Hebrew bride. An heir meant security and an elevated status for the heir's mother. Another story that demonstrates this is the story of Leah and Rachel in what I like to call the War of the Wombs.

When Rachel saw that she bore Jacob no children, she envied her sister. She said to Jacob, "Give me children, or I shall die!"

Jacob's anger was kindled against Rachel, and he said, "Am I in the place of God, who has withheld from you the fruit of the womb?"

Then she said, "Here is my servant Bilhah; go in to her, so that she may give birth on my behalf, that even I may have children through her."

So she gave him her servant Bilhah as a wife, and Jacob went in to her.

And Bilhah conceived and bore Jacob a son.

Then Rachel said, "God has judged me, and has also heard my voice and given me a son." Therefore, she called his name Dan.

Rachel's servant Bilhah conceived again and bore Jacob a second son.

Then Rachel said, "With mighty wrestlings I have wrestled with my sister and have prevailed." So she called his name Naphtali.

When Leah saw that she had ceased bearing children, she took her servant Zilpah and gave her to Jacob as a wife.

Then Leah's servant Zilpah bore Jacob a son.
And Leah said, "Good fortune has come!" so she called his name
Gad.
Leah's servant Zilpah bore Jacob a second son.
And Leah said, "Happy am I! For women have called me happy."
So she called his name Asher. (Gen 30:1-13)

For the bride, the long and short of all of this can simply be summed up by the following statement, "No heir, no inheritance!"

We have already discussed how in Hebrew culture, when a man child came of age, the father would publicly declare that he was adopting his man child as an heir. However, it's crucial to note that from the moment the covenant was made, the son became an exact image of his father. He was empowered to transact with as much authority as his father regarding issues of the family inheritance.

The father's declaration, "My child has come of age, and I am pleased with him," signified his confidence that his son would act and

speak in perfect harmony with him. The father's interests had become his son's interests; they had become one. This understanding sheds light on Jesus' response to John's reluctance to baptize Him. Jesus said, "Let it be so now, for thus it is fitting for us to fulfill all righteousness." This response was appropriate because it was only after Jesus had been baptized that the Father could publicly declare Him to be His Son.

Then Jesus came from Galilee to the Jordan to John, to be
baptized by him.
John would have prevented him, saying, "I need to be baptized by
you, and do you come to me?"

But Jesus answered him, "Let it be so now, for thus it is fitting for us to fulfill all righteousness." Then he consented.
And when Jesus was baptized, immediately he went up from the water, and behold, the heavens were opened to him, and he saw the Spirit of God descending like a dove and coming to rest on him;
and behold, a voice from heaven said, "This is my beloved Son, with whom I am well pleased." (Mat 3:13-17)

The legal precedent had been set in centuries past. A father could only declare his child as heir when the child was ready to leave childish things behind him. Jesus', baptism amongst other things was signal that he was now mature and ready to do his fathers' will for his life and as such was turning away from his former a life of caring for his mother and his earthly fathers' family in order to do his heavenly Fathers bidding. So as soon as he was baptized the Father took his signet ring, that is the Holy Spirit, and put it upon him to remain a seal of authority giving him the right to access all of his heavenly Fathers inheritance in order to transact his fathers' business. Then the God the Father himself made the announcement, "This is my beloved Son, with whom I am well pleased," before the crowd that was gathered which as the passage tells us was made up of all manner of people that included Pharisees and Sadducees; see Mat 3:7

As you can imagine Pharisees and Sadducees were considered elders in Hebrew society.

Armed with this understanding you can now understand why Jesus made statements like; "I and my Father are one", "I only do what I see my Father do" and "I only say what I hear my Father say".

"So Jesus said to them, "Truly, truly, I say to you, the Son can do nothing of his own accord, but only what he sees the Father doing. For whatever the Father does, that the Son does likewise."
(Joh 5:19)
"I and the Father are one." (Joh 10:30)

"Do you not believe that I am in the Father and the Father is in me? The words that I say to you I do not speak on my own authority, but the Father who dwells in me does his works." (Joh 14:10)

When Jesus makes these statement he was in fact affirming the sandal covenant between him as the son of God in flesh and his heavenly Father who is God over all, imagine how much this must have infuriated the Pharisees and Sadducees.

Another way in which the sandal covenant manifested itself was during the Hebrew marriage ritual when the groom would remove the sandals which the bride had worn at her father's house and walked in to his home, wash her feet and place new pair of sandals on her now clean feet. By doing this he was removing her from her father's inheritance (taking of the sandals that had walked upon her father's inheritance), wiping our away all traces of her father's inheritance hence imploring her to forget about her father's inheritance (washing of the dust of her father's inheritance from her feet) and then inviting her to be a partaker of his own inheritance (by putting now sandal upon her feet).

This is the custom of the sandal covenant according to ancient Hebraic custom.

The Covenant of Praise: A Bond of Unending Devotion

The Covenant of Praise is a profound and transformative agreement between God and His people, characterized by mutual devotion, worship, and adoration. This covenantal bond is established and sustained through the expressive language of praise, sealing a permanent relationship between the parties involved.

Key Elements of the Covenant of Praise

The Covenant of Praise is initiated and sealed through the heartfelt act of singing praises to God, acknowledging His sovereignty, goodness, and faithfulness (Psalm 103:1-5). This sacred bond is further confirmed through vows of devotion, where individuals commit to honor, worship, and obey God (Psalm 116:14-19). Ultimately, the Covenant of Praise is marked by mutual affection and loyalty between God and His people, fostering a profound sense of intimacy and connection (Psalm 138:8).

The Covenant of Praise finds powerful expression in various biblical accounts, showcasing its transformative power and beauty.

One exemplary illustration is David's heartfelt psalm in Psalm 103. This iconic prayer overflows with gratitude, adoration, and unwavering commitment to God, epitomizing the Covenant of Praise. David's words resonate with sincerity, demonstrating the depth of his relationship with God.

Another vivid demonstration of the Covenant of Praise can be seen in the Psalms of Ascent (Psalms 120-134). These sacred songs, sung by pilgrims ascending to Jerusalem, bring the Covenant of Praise to life. As travelers journeyed to the holy city, they voiced their trust, hope, and devotion to God, reflecting the mutual affection and loyalty at the heart of the covenant.

Perhaps one of the most triumphant expressions of the Covenant of Praise is Moses' song after the miraculous Red Sea crossing (Exodus 15:1-21). With Pharaoh's armies vanquished and the Israelites safely on the other shore, Moses burst into joyful song, celebrating God's deliverance and sovereignty. This majestic hymn embodies the Covenant of Praise, testifying to God's unwavering presence and power.

Ancient Hebraic Marriage Rituals and the Covenant of Praise

In Ancient Hebraic marriage rituals, the Covenant of Praise was intricately woven into the ceremony, reflecting the deep connection between God and His people:

1. Shirat HaNissuin (Wedding Song): A joyful song praising God for the gift of the bride.

2. Kiddushin (Betrothal): The groom recited blessings and praises to God, committing to honor and cherish his bride.

3. Huppah (Canopy): The couple recited prayers and praises, invoking God's presence and protection.

4. Sheva Brachot (Seven Blessings): These blessings praised God for creating joy, love, and companionship.

5. Shir HaMa'alot (Song of Ascents): Psalms 120-134 expressed gratitude and praise to God.

6. Ketubah (Marriage Contract): The ketubah included phrases praising God and acknowledging His presence in the marriage.

Implications and Significance

The Covenant of Praise:

- Emphasizes worship as a covenantal act

- Has transformative power, shaping individuals and communities

- Ensures an enduring relationship between God and His people

- Celebrates God's sovereignty and goodness

- Invokes divine blessing and protection

The Covenant of Praise stands is a testament to the profound and enduring relationship between, the husband and wife in the case of Israel, God and His people. Through the expressive language of praise, this sacred bond is initiated, sealed, and sustained, fostering a deep sense of intimacy, mutual devotion, and loyalty. As exemplified in David's psalm, the Psalms of Ascent, and Moses' triumphant song, the Covenant of Praise transcends mere worship, becoming a transformative force that shapes individuals and communities. Its presence in Ancient Hebraic marriage rituals underscores the covenantal nature of relationships, reflecting God's relational framework with His people.

References

1. Mendenhall, G. E. (1954). Covenant forms in Israelite tradition. Biblical Archaeologist, 17(3), 50-76.

2. Nicholson, E. W. (1986). *God and His People: Covenant and Theology in the Old Testament*. Oxford University Press.

3. Hillers, D. R. (1969). *Covenant: The History of a Biblical Concept*. Johns Hopkins University Press.

4. Ross, A. P. (1988). *Recalling the Covenant*. Bibliotheca Sacra, 145(578), 136-146.

Important but Secondary References

1. Stern, D. H. (1992). *Jewish New Testament Commentary*. Jewish New Testament Publications.

2. Barton, J., & Muddiman, J. (2001). *The Hebrew Bible: A Critical Companion*. Oxford University Press.

3. Eaton, J. H. (1976). *The Psalms: A Historical and Spiritual Commentary*. T. & T. Clark.

4. Hugenberger, G. P. (1994). *Marriage as Covenant*. Crossway..

Chapter 4: The Ancient Hebrew Marriage Kuddushin and Nissuin

In ancient Hebraic tradition, marriage rites were structured around two distinct yet interdependent stages: Kiddushin (betrothal or engagement) and Nissuin (marriage proper). Each stage carried profound symbolic weight and covenantal meaning, reflecting a deep, covenant-driven relationship that pointed to God's commitment to His people and vice versa. The marriage was not just a union of two individuals but a communal and sacred covenantal bond.

The Structure of the Marriage Rite

The marriage rite unfolded in two primary stages, Kiddushin and Nissuin, which included three primary processes: Contract, Consummation, and Celebration. These stages, though separate, were interconnected in forming the full marriage covenant.

Kiddushin (Betrothal)

The western equivalent to kiddushin or betrothal would be engagement even though it was more than just an engagement as we know it; it was a legally binding covenant making process that set the bride and groom apart exclusively for one another. The term "Kiddushin" derives from the Hebrew root qadosh, meaning "sanctified" or "set apart." Once Kiddushin was complete, the bride and groom were legally bound as husband and wife, and this bond could only be dissolved through divorce or death. However, they did not yet live together or fulfill their marital responsibilities until the Nissuin stage was completed. This period could last up to a year, providing time for preparation, especially for the groom, who would go to prepare a home for his bride.

The Betrothal Ceremony took place at the home of the bride's father, who formally received the groom and his father. Traditionally, upon the arrival of the groom to the bride's home the father of the bride asked the her if he should let the groom enter. Upon her approval, the groom was invited in, and the families began the process of forming the marriage covenant.

During Kiddushin, three distinct cups of wine were consumed, each representing one of the three ancient Hebrew covenants: Blood Covenant (Servanthood), Salt Covenant (Friendship), and Sandal Covenant (Inheritance). These cups were not only symbolic but helped solidify the relationship structure between the bride, groom, and their families.

The First Cup – The Blood Covenant of Servanthood in the Cup of Sanctification:

The first cup of wine, shared among both families, symbolized servanthood and the commitment to support the new family. Known as the Cup of Sanctification, it signified the setting apart of the bride and groom for one another, binding both families to support and serve one another as an extended family unit. This step underscored the sanctity and sincerity of the relationship, as "Betrothal" itself means to "Be Truthful," fostering a spirit of trust and transparency. It is important to note that the relatives of both the bride and groom partook of this cup, because the covenant extended beyond the union of the bride and groom but to their families as well.

The Second Cup – The Salt Covenant of Friendship and Hospitality in the Cup of Dedication:

The second cup, shared only by the bride, groom, and their fathers, represented friendship, hospitality, and loyalty. It followed the negotiation of the Ketubah, the marriage contract. This cup, known as the Cup of Dedication, symbolized loyalty and was central to the covenant-making process, often involving the sharing of salt as a binding act. Each family member mixed their salt in a communal dish, symbolizing eternal friendship, as the salt grains would forever be intermingled.

The Third Cup – The Sandal Covenant of Inheritance in the Cup of Redemption:

The final cup of the Kiddushin, the Cup of Redemption, was shared solely by the bride and groom. Drinking from this cup sealed the covenant between them and marked the end of the Kiddushin process, signifying their mutual commitment. Traditionally, this was also the point at which the Ketubah was formally signed and finalized by a scribe, making the marriage official in the community's eyes. The Ketubah document itself was highly symbolic, reflecting the structure of the Torah and containing five parts: genealogy of the couple, family histories, their courtship story, and their mutual responsibilities.

After the Kiddushin, the groom departed to prepare a place for his bride, typically at his father's house. The bride, in turn, would ready herself for his return, preparing her attire and keeping herself set apart, symbolizing purity and devotion.

Nissuin (Marriage Proper)
The Nissuin, meaning "elevation or lifting up," marked the completion and consummation of the marriage. Unlike

Kiddushin, which was largely focused on contractual obligations, Nissuin was celebratory, signifying the full union of the bride and groom. Nissuin could only begin after the groom's father declared the home ready, which could be months or even a year later.

The Groom's Return:

The groom's return to the bride's house was a highly anticipated event, usually occurring at night. The groom, accompanied by a joyful procession of friends, would sound a shofar (ram's horn) to announce his arrival. The surprise timing highlighted the bride's readiness, underscoring her devotion and commitment to wait for her groom's return.

The Wedding Feast and Chuppah:

Once the bride joined the groom, they traveled to the groom's home, where they celebrated under the Chuppah (wedding canopy). The Chuppah represented the new home they would build together and was a place of blessing, with the couple receiving prayers and blessings from family and community.

The Fourth Cup – The Covenant of Praise in The Cup of Praise or Blessing:

During the feast, the bride and groom shared a fourth cup of wine, the Cup of Praise, sealing the covenant of marriage. The Cup of Praise, also called the Cup of Blessing, was the final act of covenant-making, symbolizing the completion of the marriage vows. They also partook of Challah bread, dipped in salt, in remembrance of the Salt Covenant, solidifying their bond of friendship.

Consummation of the Marriage:

After the feast, the bride and groom would consummate the marriage, finalizing their union physically in a private setting. This intimate act was the ultimate sealing of the covenant and marked the fulfillment of the marriage relationship.

The Hebrew marriage customs symbolized deep spiritual truths. The Kiddushin represented the covenant between God and His people, with the three covenants (Servanthood, Friendship, Inheritance) illustrating the roles and responsibilities within this sacred relationship. Just as the groom prepared a home for the bride, God was seen as preparing a place for His people, and like the bride, His people were called to be ready, living in faithful expectation. The Nissuin foretold the snatching away of another bride the church in the far future by her groom (Jesus the Christ) from a corrupt, condemned and perishing world.

Parallels to Covenant with God and Scriptural Significance

The entire structure of the marriage rite — from Kiddushin to Nissuin, the Ketubah to the cups of wine — reflects the divine covenant God has with His people. The Torah, or Pentateuch, echoes this in its structure, functioning as a kind of "Ketubah" that outlines the sacred relationship between God and humanity. Many scholars draw parallels between these marriage customs and passages in the Bible, especially in the New Testament, where marriage is frequently used as a metaphor for the relationship between Christ and the Church (e.g., Matthew 25:1–13; John 14:1–3; Ephesians 5:25–27).

These marriage rites convey the sanctity, loyalty, and eternal commitment expected within marriage, transforming a simple union into a living reflection of divine covenant.

References

1. Kiddushin (Betrothal) and Nissuin (Marriage Proper):
    - "The Jewish Wedding" by Maurice Lamm (2004)
    - "The Encyclopedia of Jewish Prayer" by Macy Nulman (1993)
    2. The Three Cups of Wine:
    - "The Jewish Wedding" by Maurice Lamm (2004)
    - "The Book of Jewish Knowledge" by Nathan Ausubel (1964)
    3. Ketubah (Marriage Contract):
    - "The Jewish Wedding" by Maurice Lamm (2004)
    - "The Encyclopedia of Jewish Prayer" by Macy Nulman (1993)
    4. Nissuin (Marriage Proper) and the Chuppah:
    - "The Jewish Wedding" by Maurice Lamm (2004)
    - "The Book of Jewish Knowledge" by Nathan Ausubel (1964)
    5. Parallels to Covenant with God and Scriptural Significance:
    - "The Bible and the Jewish Wedding" by Michael L. Satlow (2014)
    - "The Jewish Study Bible" edited by Adele Berlin and Marc Zvi Brettler (2004)

Chapter 5: The Kiddushin, God and Abraham negotiate Israel's' betrothal

Within the story of Abraham and God, we see an early foreshadowing of this betrothal process: God, as the divine Father, initiates a covenant with Abraham, father of Israel. This covenant is the foundation of a profound relationship—a divine ketubah—that will one day unite God with His people as Bridegroom and Bride. Through promises of redemption, inheritance, and eternal love, God's covenant with Abraham mirrors the very elements of a marriage agreement, binding Israel to Himself in an everlasting union. Each section in this chapter traces a progression in this covenant relationship, one that reflects the stages of a betrothal as God and Abraham, in their paternal roles, prepare for a future Bride and Groom to come together in sacred unity.

The Third Cup – Redeemed unto God

In the ancient Hebrew marriage betrothal ceremony, the third cup, known as the Cup of Redemption, symbolized the completion of the betrothal process. This cup was shared between the bride and groom at the end of the betrothal meal, marking the seal of their covenant. The scribe would finalize the ketubah—the marriage contract. Once the contract was signed, the couple was legally bound, recognized by the community as husband and wife, though they had not yet consummated their union.

This practice sheds light on God's unfolding covenant with Israel, initiated through Abraham. The story of Abraham, Isaac, and Jacob illustrates God's enduring promises, even, through hardship. In Genesis, God reveals to Abraham both the blessings and trials that would come upon his descendants.

Then the LORD said to Abram, "Know for certain that your offspring will be sojourners in a land that is not theirs and will be servants there, and they will be afflicted for four hundred years.

But I will bring judgment on the nation that they serve, and afterward they shall come out with great possessions.

As for you, you shall go to your fathers in peace; you shall be buried in a good old age.

And they shall come back here in the fourth generation, for the iniquity of the Amorites is not yet complete." (Genesis 15:13-16, ESV).

This prophecy of affliction foretold Israel's bondage in Egypt, yet it also carried the promise of deliverance. In Exodus, God remembers this covenant and prepares to fulfill His promises by redeeming Israel:

"And God heard their groaning, and God remembered his covenant with Abraham, with Isaac, and with Jacob. God saw the people of Israel—and God knew" (Exodus 2:23-25, ESV).

This betrothal-type covenant, with its promise of redemption, reflects God's faithful love and commitment to Abraham and his descendants. As God's covenant unfolds, it is like the betrothal cup that signifies a binding commitment, leading His people toward liberation and relationship with Him.

Isaac's Redemption as a Sandal Covenant

The story of Isaac's near-sacrifice by Abraham marks a significant act of redemption. When God commands Abraham to offer Isaac as a burnt offering, He introduces a substitutionary redemption that deeply impacts Isaac and his lineage. As Abraham is about to sacrifice Isaac, God intervenes, providing a ram as a substitute. Through this act, God purchases Isaac, claiming Isaac's life and, by extension, his descendants as His own. From that moment on, Isaac and his lineage are bound to God as a bondservant to a master.

The bondservant principle in Exodus reinforces this relationship. According to Mosaic law, if the master of a bondservant gave him a wife to he reserved the right to claim the children as his own.

If thou shalt buy a Hebrew servant, six years he shall serve: and in the seventh he shall depart free for nothing.
If he came in by himself, he shall depart by himself: if he was married, then his wife shall depart with him.
If his master hath given him a wife, and she hath borne him sons or daughters; the wife and her children shall be her master's, and he shall depart by himself.
(Ex. 21:2-4)

So God, by redeeming Isaac and giving him a wife through his response to the prayers of Eleazar (Genesis 24), also claims Isaac's descendants. This relationship is later seen in God's declaration,

"Israel my servant, Jacob whom I have chosen" (Isaiah 41:8-9).

Through Isaac's redemption, God reaffirms with Isaac the covenant of servanthood and inheritance which he established with Abraham. This relationship foreshadows Israel's own redemption from Egyptian slavery, where God again intervenes as Redeemer. With the Passover lamb's blood marking their homes, Israel is consecrated to God. Thus, the sandal covenant binds Isaac's lineage to God, as Israel becomes His chosen people through a covenant relationship of redemption and inheritance.

The Sandal Covenant of Sonship/Inheritance

The concept of the sandal covenant represents authority, dominion, and inheritance, which God bestows upon Abraham and his descendants. When God tells Abraham to "walk through the length and breadth of the land, for I am giving it to you" (Genesis 13:17, ESV), it is more than a command to explore—it is a symbolic act of claiming dominion over the land. This form of a "sandal covenant" reflects ownership and inheritance, a promise that extends through Abraham's lineage.

God's covenant with Abraham deepens in Genesis 17, where He promises that Abraham will be "a father of many nations" and grants an "everlasting possession" to his offspring. This covenant ensures that Abraham's descendants will inherit the land and fulfill a divinely ordained purpose. This inheritance and sonship is rooted in the relationship established between Abraham and God, a relationship that becomes foundational for Israel's identity.

In the sandal covenant of inheritance, we see the importance of covenantal relationships, not just as promises but as relational bonds. This covenant is given to Abraham, Isaac, and Jacob and later reaffirmed to Israel. It binds them to God, setting them apart as His chosen people—a people defined by a relationship of love, redemption, and divine inheritance. In this chapter, we witness the unfolding of God's covenant as both a legal and relational bond, comparable to the ancient betrothal process. The betrothal cup, Isaac's redemption, and the sandal covenant illustrate a progression from commitment to inheritance, as God prepares Israel to become His people and inherit His promises. This chapter portrays the depth of God's love and His dedication to His people, whom He redeems and claims as His own through covenant

References

Stern, D. H. (1992). The Hebrew Marriage Covenant. Jewish New Testament Publications.

Wenham, G. J. (1998). Genesis 1-15. Word Biblical Commentary.

Chapter 6: The Passover –A picture of Nissuin (Elevation) as God Comes for His Bride

Unveiling the Nissuin Phase

In the ancient Hebrew wedding custom, the Nissuin phase represents the culmination of the marriage process. This final stage symbolizes the consummation of the union between God and Israel. A fascinating parallel emerges when examining the Exodus narrative, particularly the events surrounding Passover.

A Divine Courtship

As the Israelites prepared to leave Egypt, they received jewelry and clothing from the Egyptians (Exodus 12:35-36), reminiscent of Eleazer adorning Rebekah with jewelry before taking her to Isaac (Genesis 24:53). This act symbolizes the groom's provision for his bride. God, the divine Groom, demonstrated His love and care for Israel.

Crossing the Threshold

God's dramatic deliverance of Israel through the Red Sea (Exodus 14:13-31) washed the feet of the Israelites, symbolizing their transition from slavery to freedom and their new inheritance (Exodus 14:13-14). This echoes the custom of the groom washing the bride's feet before taking her to the bridal chamber.

A Song of Praise

After crossing the Red Sea, the Israelites sang a song of praise (Exodus 15:1-21), mirroring the fourth Cup of Praise in the Hebrew marriage ritual. This song celebrates God's redemption and deliverance.

Covenant at Sinai

The culmination of the Nissuin phase occurs at Mount Sinai, where God and Israel exchange vows (Exodus 19-24). God promises to make Israel a treasured possession, a kingdom of priests, and a holy nation (Exodus 19:5-6). In response, Israel vows to obey God's voice and keep His covenant (Exodus 24:7).

The Priesthood and Tabernacle

The priesthood, established at Sinai, represents the bride who was the subject of the marriage. God's desire, when He entered into covenant with Abraham, was for his offspring to be a blessing to the nations (Genesis 22:15-18). This blessing was to bring the nations to a saving knowledge of God.

A Kingdom of Priests

God's intention was for every Israelite to serve Him as a priest, with the mandate of bringing the greatest blessing possible to humanity – reconciling humanity to Himself (Exodus 19:5-6). However, the Golden Calf incident altered this plan. When Israel approached Aaron and asked him to make a god for them to worship i.e. the Golden Calf (Exodus 32), they breached their covenant vows, mirroring the consequences of adultery in a marriage. God would have destroyed the whole nation but Moses like the best man interceded on Israel's behalf (Exodus 32:11-14) and God relented, however there were consequences for Israel's infidelity.

When Moses came back from his meeting with God and he saw what the Israelites had done he simply asked, "Who is on the Lords side?" and the sons of Levi gathered around him. What Moses said next will bring into sharp perspective how seriously covenant was viewed in ancient Hebraic and indeed eastern culture.

Moses said to them,

" Thus says the LORD God of Israel, 'Put your sword on your side each of you, and go to and fro from gate to gate throughout the camp, and each of you kill his brother and his companion and his neighbor." (Exodus 32:27),

The sons of Levi did what Moses instructed them to do, and around three thousand people died that day.

The Priesthood, a Marriage Covenant in the Fourth Cup of Praise

As a result of Israel's infidelity, God adapted His plan. The Levites, who chose God and executed his judgement, choosing God and justice over their kin, were ordained to serve as priests (Exodus 32:25-29). Because there was a breach in covenant relationship between God and the nation of Israel the Levites in their role of priest, the bride of God assumed the role of mediator between God and Israel and Gods original plan to have a priesthood that would mediate between him and all mankind was put on hold but not derailed. However, as priests of the Lord God they enjoyed special intimacy with God and were privileged to have the honor of serving in the tabernacle fulfilling a role that is similar to the one that Abraham played in the events leading up to the destruction of Sodom and the salvation of Lot and reminiscent of how the Jewish bride relates with her husband.

The ordination of the Levites, their priestly garments, and the tabernacle reflect Nissuin themes, as Israel steps into a sacred bond with God as His "bride."

1. Consecration and Purification: A Bride Set Apart

In the Nissuin stage, a bride prepares herself in purity for her groom. This act of consecration mirrors Israel's own purification before receiving the Law at Sinai (Exodus 19:10-15).

Like a bride entering covenant, Israel's washing of clothes and abstention from impurity signified readiness for sacred union. The Levites, too, underwent purification—ritual shaving, washing, and sprinkling (Numbers 8:5-7)—in preparation for their ordination. These actions paralleled the bride's sanctification, setting them apart as mediators in Israel's divine covenant.

2. Priestly Garments: Adornments of the Bride

The holy garments of the priests and the high priest mirror a bride's symbolic adornments, marking Israel's status as God's beloved. The priests wore intricate ephods, breastplates with stones representing the tribes, and a "crown of holiness" (Exodus 28:4-5, 39:30-31), reflecting honor and consecration. This attire symbolizes Israel's beauty, set apart for divine service, just as a bride's garments represent her sanctity and devotion. The high priest's breastplate, bearing the tribes over his heart, illustrates God's remembrance of Israel—similar to a groom holding his bride close to his heart.

3. Anointing: A Symbol of Covenant Union

In Nissuin, the bride's anointing with oil symbolizes her dedication to her groom. In parallel, the anointing of the Levites (Exodus 29:7) signified their consecration to God, marking them as a people set apart for divine union and service. This anointing with oil represents spiritual communion, much as the bride's anointing prepares her for her husband.

4. The Tabernacle: God's Dwelling Place as a Bridal Chamber

The tabernacle, designed meticulously to God's specifications, symbolizes the bridal chamber—the intimate dwelling where God would meet His bride, Israel (Exodus 25:8). The materials—linen, goat hair, and red-dyed ram skins—each carry profound symbolism: linen for purity, goat hair for protection, and ram skins for sacrificial love – as in the case of Isaacs redemption (Exodus 26:1; Leviticus 4:25; Exodus 29:21). The Holy of Holies, like the bride and groom's private space, remained veiled and accessible only to the high priest, reinforcing the exclusivity of Israel's relationship with God.

5. Covenant as Marriage Contract (Ketubah) and Priestly Mediation

At Sinai, God formalized His covenant with Israel—a spiritual marriage contract. This "ketubah" echoed the promise of a treasured union (Exodus 24:7). As Israel's covenant with God became official, the Levites assumed the role of bride, priestly mediators, like Queen Esther acting as mediators for members of their family, Moses acting as the (friend of the groom) facilitating the marriage, supporting the relationship between the priesthood and God. This intermediary role assumed by the Levites on behalf of the Israelites was a far cry from what God originally had in mind for the nation of Israel, but became a foreshadowing the coming of the "kingdom of priests" (Exodus 19:6) that had been put on hold but was still to come. Thus revealing God's intent to include all nations in His covenant family.

6. The Seven-Day Consecration: A Wedding Celebration

The seven-day ordination of the Levites paralleled the seven-day wedding celebration of Nissuin. This consecration period signified a dedication to divine service, much like the wedding celebration dedicates the bride and groom to one another. During these seven days, sacrifices served as offerings of dedication and purity, aligning with the bride's sacrificial love and commitment in marriage (Exodus 29:35-37; Ezekiel 43:25-27).

7. The Betrothal Cup of Praise and the Altar of Incense

In Nissuin, the fourth cup of praise, or Cup of Blessing, represents the marriage covenant's culmination. This cup, echoed in the ordination rituals (Exodus 29:42-46), welcomed Aaron and his sons into God's inheritance, symbolizing Israel's acceptance into divine fellowship. The altar of incense, placed before the veil, signified intimacy with God through prayer (Exodus 30:1-6). Its incense, symbolizing the prayers of saints (Psalm 141:2; Revelation 5:8), reinforced the relational closeness God desires with His people.

8. Urim and Thummim: Guiding the Bride's Path

The high priest's breastplate contained the Urim and Thummim, which provided divine guidance (Exodus 28:30). This guidance represents God's commitment to leading Israel, akin to a groom's protective care over his bride. These stones reflect God's light and perfection, revealing His will for Israel, who, as His bride, is called to walk in covenantal faithfulness.

Conclusion: A Sacred Union in the Sanctuary

The consecration of Aaron and his sons, the tabernacle's construction, and the priestly garments reveal the depth of God's covenantal relationship with Israel, His "bride." The sanctuary's design serves as a symbolic bridal chamber, embodying the covenant of love and dedication. This sacred union is reinforced in the betrothal cup, the priestly adornment, and the tabernacle rituals, establishing Israel's role as God's beloved partner in a covenant that points to ultimate redemption and union with God.

References

Frymer-Kensky, T. (1992). In the Wake of the Goddesses: Women, Culture, and the Biblical Transformation of Pagan Myth. Fawcett Columbine.

Hillers, D. R. (1969). Covenant: The History of a Biblical Idea. Johns Hopkins University Press.

Levenson, J. D. (1992). The Hebrew Bible, the Old Testament, and Historical Criticism: Jews and Christians in Biblical Studies. Westminster John Knox Press.

Fesko, J. V. (2018). The Tabernacle: Its Structure and Symbolism.

Rodriguez, A. M. (2015). The Priestly Garments.

Hartley, J. E. (1992). The Urim and Thummim

Chapter 7: Unto us, a child is born, Jesus the fulfillment of the covenant

In the preceding chapters, we uncovered the profound connections between ancient Hebrew marriage customs and God's covenantal relationship with Israel. This journey began with the Kiddushin phase, explored in Chapter 5, where God initiated a betrothal covenant with Abraham. This divine commitment promised redemption, inheritance, and eternal love, mirroring the elements of a marriage agreement and binding Israel to God in an everlasting union.

Chapter 6 then revealed the Nissuin phase, where God consummated His union with Israel through the Exodus, Passover, and the giving of the Law at Sinai. The intricate details of this phase, including the ordination of the Levites, the tabernacle's design, and the priestly garments, all reflected the themes of consecration, purification, and adornment found in ancient Hebrew wedding customs. Through these chapters, we have seen that:

- God's covenant with Abraham established a divine ketubah, a marriage contract that bound Israel to Him.
- The betrothal cup, Isaac's redemption, and the sandal covenant illustrated God's commitment to Israel.
- The Exodus and Passover mirrored the Nissuin phase, symbolizing God's deliverance and union with Israel.
- The tabernacle and priestly garments represented the bridal chamber and adornments of Israel, God's

beloved.

- The Levites' ordination and the covenant at Sinai formalized Israel's role as a kingdom of priests.

As we transition to the New Testament, we'll discover how Jesus' life, teachings, and ultimate sacrifice remarkably mirror the ancient Hebrew ketubah as well. We'll explore how Jesus' covenant with His original disciples represents a new and distinct marriage covenant, one that expands God's plan of redemption to encompass all nations. At the heart of this plan is Jesus, the Son of God, who embodies the role of the divine Bridegroom, while also being the Son of the bride, humanity.

A Child is born

And there appeared a great wonder in heaven; a woman clothed with the sun, and the moon under her feet, and upon her head a crown of twelve stars:
And she being with child, cried, travailing in birth, and pained to be delivered.
And there appeared another wonder in heaven; and behold, a great red dragon, having seven heads and ten horns, and seven crowns upon his heads.
And his tail drew the third part of the stars of heaven, and cast them to the earth: and the dragon stood before the woman who was ready to be delivered, to devour her child as soon as it was born.
And she brought forth a male child, who was to rule all nations with a rod of iron: and her child was caught up to God, and to his throne. (Rev, 12:1-5)

MYSTERY OF THE TWO COVENANTS

There is nothing that gives a bride as much joy as giving birth to a son that will inherit all that the groom owns. This joy is echoed in the prophetic words of Isaiah;

Nevertheless, the dimness shall not be such as was in her distress, when at the first he lightly afflicted the land of Zebulun, and the land of Naphtali, and afterward did more grievously afflict her by the way of the sea, beyond Jordan, in Galilee of the nations.

The people that walked in darkness have seen a great light: they that dwell in the land of the shades of death, upon them hath the light shined.

Thou hast multiplied the nation, and not increased the joy: they joy before thee according to the joy in harvest, and as men rejoice when they divide the spoil.

For thou hast broken the yoke of his burden, and the staff of his shoulder, the rod of his oppressor, as in the day of Midian.

For every battle of the warrior is with confused noise, and garments rolled in blood; but this shall be with burning and fuel of fire.

For to us a child is born, to us a son is given: and the government shall be upon his shoulder: and his name shall be called Wonderful, Counselor, The mighty God, The everlasting Father, The Prince of Peace.

Of the increase of his government and peace there shall be no end, upon the throne of David, and upon his kingdom, to order it, and to establish it with judgment and with justice from henceforth even forever. The zeal of the LORD of hosts will perform this. (Isa 9:1-7)

Every bride is expected to bear a son; would we expect the bride of God to do any less? Since marriage is an institution ordained by God, it's reasonable to assume that He would observe His own institution when causing a woman to give birth to His Son.

When God entered into a marriage covenant with Abraham, paying a dowry of a ram on Mount Moriah, and when He gave Israel a token of jewelry as she left Egypt, bringing her into the Promised Land, He had a virgin child in mind. A child who would be born of His Spirit, overshadowing a virgin, Mary. This child would be Jesus Christ, the second Adam, who would restore all things to their original state.

Mary, as the bride of God, was the one for whom God paid the bride price on Mount Moriah. Therefore, when the prophet Isaiah declares, "Unto us a child is born, unto us a son is given" (Isaiah 9:6), he speaks on behalf of Israel, the family of God's bride. These words are those of a proud uncle, anticipating the arrival of his nephew, who would restore the destiny of not only Israel but all humanity.

Indeed, there was great cause for celebration, for the birth of the heir of the Groom secured Israel's inheritance forever! The advent of the Christ, the heir of God, was foretold in Scripture from the beginning of human history (Gen 3:15(.

I am convinced that the Abrahamic and Mosaic Covenants, as well as the Law of the Old Testament, represent a marriage contract negotiation between God and Abraham. This covenant granted God the right to have a son born on earth through Mary, and its fulfillment came with the birth of Jesus. Passed down to the Jewish nation, this covenant was observed throughout the ages.

The Bible clearly indicates that Jesus is the ultimate fulfillment of the Abrahamic and Mosaic Covenants, which reached their culmination in the Nissuin phase with the giving of the Law. Jesus Himself confirmed this, revealing the true nature of God's relationship with His people.

Think not that I am come to destroy the law, or the prophets: I am not come to destroy, but to fulfill.

For verily I say to you, till heaven and earth shall pass away, one jot or one tittle shall in no wise pass from the law, till all be fulfilled.

Whoever therefore shall break one of these least commandments, and shall teach men so, he shall be called the least in the kingdom of heaven: but whoever shall do, and teach them, the same shall be called great in the kingdom of heaven.

For I say to you, that except your righteousness shall exceed the righteousness of the scribes and Pharisees, ye shall in no case enter into the kingdom of heaven. (Mat 5:17-20)

Jesus' statement emphasizes that He is the fulfillment of the Law, and His arrival marks the completion of the Abrahamic Covenant. He is the manifestation of the covenant and its law, and as such, not even the smallest detail of the Law has been or will be done away with.

The wisdom of God is truly amazing, as He entered into a ketubah covenant with Abraham to claim His bride (Mary) and cause her to give birth to Jesus, God's heir on earth, for the salvation of mankind. This idea is echoed by Paul in his letter to the Romans (Chapter 10).

For Christ is the end of the law for righteousness to everyone who believes. (Rom 10:1-4)) ESV

"For Christ is the end of the law [it leads to Him and its purpose is fulfilled in Him], for [granting] righteousness to everyone who believes [in Him as Savior]".

(Rom 10 v 4) AMP

Paul reiterates this fact again in Galatians and this time discusses it at length, and I really believe that we should pay close attention to the import of his words.

To give a human example, brothers: even with a man-made covenant, no one annuls it or adds to it once it has been ratified. Now the promises were made to Abraham and to his offspring. It does not say, "And to offsprings," referring to many, but referring to one, "And to your offspring," who is Christ.

This is what I mean: the law, which came 430 years afterward, does not annul a covenant previously ratified by God, so as to make the promise void.

For if the inheritance comes by the law, it no longer comes by promise; but God gave it to Abraham by a promise.

Why then the law? It was added because of transgressions, until the offspring should come to whom the promise had been made, and it was put in place through angels by an intermediary. Now an intermediary implies more than one, but God is one. Is the law then contrary to the promises of God? Certainly not! For if a law had been given that could give life, then righteousness would indeed be by the law.

But the Scripture imprisoned everything under sin, so that the promise by faith in Jesus Christ might be given to those who believe.

Now before faith came, we were held captive under the law, imprisoned until the coming faith would be revealed. So then, the law was our guardian until Christ came, in order that we might be justified by faith. But now that faith has come, we are no longer under a guardian, for in Christ Jesus you are all sons of God, through faith.

MYSTERY OF THE TWO COVENANTS

For as many of you as were baptized into Christ have put on Christ.
(Gal 3:15-27)
In this passage Paul makes four very bold claims;

- The promises made to Abraham were for the benefit of the coming Christ, Jesus – "Now the promises [in the covenants] were decreed to Abraham and to his seed. God does not say, "And to seeds (descendants, heirs)," as if [referring] to many [persons], but as to one, "And to your Seed," who is [none other than] Christ"

- The Law was a contract between God and Israel – "but the Law was a contract between two, God and Israel; its validity depended on both"]. What was this contract? It was a marriage (ketubah) contract between God and Israel.

- The law was never designed for the impartation of righteousness that leads to salvation, rather it provided an avenue for sin to consolidate its hold on creation – "For if a system of law had been given which could impart life, then righteousness (right standing with God) would actually have been based on law. But the Scripture has imprisoned everyone [everything—the entire world] under sin,"

- The law teaches us to recognize the messiah so that we may believe in him and be saved, because it's only the messiah who has fulfilled the law and hence has received the inheritance- "the Law has become our tutor and our disciplinarian to guide us to Christ, so that we may be justified [that is, declared free of the guilt of sin and its penalty, and placed in right standing with God] by faith. But now that faith has come, we are no longer under [the control and authority of] a tutor and disciplinarian". Now that the terms of the contract have been fulfilled has come we are no longer under the tutelage of the law, or rather we are no longer subject to the terms of Gods ketubah contract with Israel.

Since the fall of humanity in the Garden of Eden, God's ultimate desire has been to redeem the entire earth and its nations. He aims to restore humanity to its original state in the Garden, allowing Him to engage with us as members of His eternal family.

The Abrahamic Covenant and the subsequent Law of Moses, while significant, have limitations. They primarily guarantee a physical inheritance for Israel alone. However, their deeper purpose was threefold:

- To facilitate the entrance of Christ, the life-giver, into the world.
- To guarantee an earthly inheritance for Israel.
- To reveal God's nature, holiness, and humanity's inadequacy before Him, thereby highlighting the need for a Savior.

Despite accomplishing its purposes, the Law was never intended to restore humanity to righteousness due to the inherent heart condition of fallen man, including Abraham.

Consequently, the Law will always fall short in producing the fruits of righteousness in fallen humanity.

This brings us full circle back to John the Baptist's provocative declaration:

"You brood of vipers! Who warned you to flee from the wrath to come?" (Matthew 3:7, Luke 3:7)

John's stern warning underscores the inadequacy of the Law in producing true righteousness. Despite their outward adherence to the Law, the Pharisees and Sadducees were still far from genuine righteousness, prompting John's scathing rebuke. John the Baptist's message was clear: "Bear fruits in keeping with repentance... Every tree that does not bear good fruit is cut down and thrown into the fire" (Luke 3:8-9). He emphasized that being born into Abraham's bloodline under the Old Covenant did not automatically guarantee righteousness.

Abraham's righteousness was not based on his ancestry or observance of the law, but on his faith and obedience to God, which preceded the covenant. In contrast, the Jews of John's time observed the law, but their outward compliance did not change the inward condition of their hearts. Righteousness, however, is a measure of the heart's condition. A paradigm shift was necessary – a new covenant that would enable God to transform the human heart. This is precisely what God promised through the prophet Ezekiel:

"I will give you a new heart and put a new spirit in you; I will remove from you your heart of stone and give you a heart of flesh. And I will put my Spirit in you and move you to follow my decrees and be careful to keep my laws" (Ezekiel 36:26-27).

Chapter 8: The Prophets speak –

Transitioning from the Old to the New

Introduction

A common misconception among religious individuals, including the Jewish establishment in John the Baptists day, is that Abraham's righteousness was a direct result of the covenant with God. This perspective often leads to an overemphasis on performance, where one's righteousness is measured by their adherence to rules and regulations. However, this understanding is misguided. In reality, God would never enter into a covenant with someone He considers unrighteous. Abraham's righteousness was not a product of the covenant, but rather a prerequisite for it. God justified Abraham before establishing the covenant, demonstrating that justification precedes consecration.

The Mosaic law, while intended to guide Israel's relationship with God, inadvertently encouraged a superficial performance culture. By focusing on outward obedience to rules and regulations, the law created a system where righteousness was measured by one's ability to keep the law, rather than by the condition of their heart. This led to a culture of external compliance, where individuals prioritized appearances over genuine righteousness.

John the Baptist's mission marked a pivotal moment in history, bridging the Abrahamic (Old) Covenant era and the Messianic (New) Covenant era. His role was to prepare the way for Jesus, the central figure of the new covenant. This new covenant would revolutionize humanity's relationship with God, shifting the focus from external obedience to internal transformation.

Jesus Himself hinted at the imminence of this new covenant. When John the Baptist's disciples

inquired about Jesus' disciples not fasting, Jesus' response suggested that a new era was dawning. The old covenant, with its emphasis on outward performance, was giving way to a new covenant that prioritized the transformation of the heart.

In this new covenant, genuine righteousness would take precedence over superficial performance. The relationship between God and humanity would become deeper and more intimate, characterized by mutual love, trust, and commitment. This fundamental shift would redefine the way people related to God, moving from a focus on external rituals to a focus on internal transformation and heartfelt devotion.

And Jesus said to them, Can the children of the bride-chamber mourn, as long as the bridegroom is with them? but the days will come, when the bridegroom shall be taken from them, and then they will fast.

No man putteth a piece of new cloth to an old garment: for that which is put in to fill it up, taketh from the garment, and the rent is made worse.

Neither do men put new wine into old bottles: else the bottles break, and the wine runneth out, and the bottles perish: but they put new wine into new bottles, and both are preserved. (Mat 9:15-17)

Jesus' statement about the old and new wineskins was more than just a metaphor; it was a profound announcement about the nature of the new covenant He was introducing. The old wineskin represented the existing Jewish legal system, with its intricate network of laws and regulations. However, this system was inadequate to contain the new, vibrant, and dynamic reality of the Kingdom of God that Jesus was ushering in.

The new wine, which represented the teachings, principles, and power of the Kingdom, required a new and flexible container that could accommodate its explosive growth and transformative power. The old wineskin, with its rigid and inflexible structure, would inevitably burst under the pressure of the new wine, causing both to be lost.

In essence, Jesus was saying that the old covenant, with its emphasis on external obedience to laws and regulations, was insufficient to contain the new reality of the Kingdom. A new covenant, with its own distinct framework and principles, was necessary to facilitate the explosive growth and transformative power of the Kingdom.

By calling Himself the bridegroom, Jesus was also hinting at the nature of this new covenant. The imagery of marriage and betrothal was deeply rooted in Jewish culture and scripture, and Jesus was using this imagery to convey the idea that the new covenant would be a deeply personal and intimate relationship between God and humanity.

Jesus' reference to Himself as the bridegroom hinted at the intimate and personal nature of the new covenant. This perspective was echoed in the parables He shared with the crowds, which consistently conveyed the idea of a treasure of great value being selected from among lesser valuable items.

kingdom of heaven is like something precious buried in a field, which a man found and hid again; then in his joy he goes and sells all he has and buys that field.
Again the kingdom of heaven is like a man who is a dealer in search of fine and precious pearls,
Who, on finding a single pearl of great price, went and sold all he had and bought it.
Again, the kingdom of heaven is like a dragnet which was cast into the sea and gathered in fish of every sort.
When it was full, men dragged it up on the beach, and sat down and sorted out the good fish into baskets, but the worthless ones they threw away.
So it will be at the close and consummation of the age. The angels will go forth and separate the wicked from the righteous (those who are upright and in right standing with God)
And cast them [the wicked] into the furnace of fire; there will be weeping and wailing and grinding of teeth.
Have you understood all these things [parables] taken together? They said to Him, Yes, Lord.
He said to them, Therefore, every teacher and interpreter of the Sacred Writings who has been instructed about and trained for the kingdom of heaven and has become a disciple is like a householder who brings forth out of his storehouse treasure that is new and [treasure that is] old [the fresh as well as the familiar].
(Matt 13:44-52)

In the parables of the hidden treasure, the pearl of great price, and the dragnet, Jesus illustrated the kingdom of heaven as a precious and valuable reality that requires sacrifice and discernment to obtain. The parables also highlighted the distinction between the righteous and the wicked, emphasizing that the new covenant would bring about a separation between those who are upright and those who are not.

When Jesus asked His disciples if they understood these parables, they replied that they did. He then explained that a teacher of the kingdom of heaven is like a householder who brings forth both new and old treasure, indicating that the new covenant would build upon the old while introducing new and fresh realities.

Likewise, Jesus' Last Supper with His disciples was a pivotal moment in history, marking the transition from the old covenant to the new. This deliberate and symbolic meal sealed a new relationship between Jesus, the Son, and His bride, the Church. In Jewish tradition, meals were often used to seal covenants or agreements. Therefore, when Jesus shared the Last Supper with His disciples, He was using this meal to establish a new covenant with them.

This new covenant, foretold by prophets Isaiah and Jeremiah, differed significantly from the old covenant between God the Father and Israel. The old covenant was based on the law, emphasizing external obedience and ritual purity. In contrast, the new covenant was based on faith, love, and the transformation of the heart.

As Jesus shared the bread and wine with His disciples, He symbolically inaugurated this new covenant. This moment marked the beginning of a new relationship between Jesus and humanity, characterized by intimacy, love, and mutual commitment. This relationship would no longer be defined by external obedience to rules and regulations, but by a deep, inner transformation.

MYSTERY OF THE TWO COVENANTS

The apostle Paul later wrote, "Christ is the mediator of a new covenant, that those who are called may receive the promised eternal inheritance" (Hebrews 9:15). The Last Supper was a pivotal moment in this process, marking the transition from the old covenant to the new and establishing a new relationship between Jesus and humanity.

The Old Covenant: Abraham and Mary

The old covenant, initially established with Abraham (Genesis 15:9-21), ultimately served a greater purpose: to bring forth the Messiah through Mary, the Mother of Jesus. Mary, as the symbolic bride of the old covenant, gave birth to the Son who would establish the new covenant.

The prophet Hosea vividly captures the transition from the old covenant to the new covenant, using the metaphor of marriage.

In his book Hosea, the prophet uses a powerful metaphor to describe the relationship between God and Israel. He portrays God as a husband and Israel as His wife, emphasizing the intimate and covenantal nature of their relationship.

However, this marriage is marked by turmoil and infidelity. Israel, the wife, has committed spiritual adultery by turning away from God and pursuing other loves, such as idolatry and immorality. God, the husband, is deeply grieved and angry, feeling betrayed by His wife's unfaithfulness.

Through Hosea's prophecies, God expresses His disappointment and anger, saying, "She has not acknowledged that I was the one who gave her the grain, the new wine, and the olive oil, and who lavished on her silver and gold— which they used for Baal" (Hosea 2:8). These words convey the pain and hurt of a loving God who has been rejected by His people.

Despite this tumultuous relationship, Hosea's prophecies also point to a future time of restoration and redemption. God promises to renew His covenant with Israel, to forgive her infidelity, and to restore their relationship. This promise is fulfilled in the new covenant established through Jesus Christ, which brings about a new era of intimacy and relationship between God and humanity.

"Say to your brothers, "You are my people," and to your sisters, "You have received mercy."

Plead with your mother, plead— for she is not my wife, and I am not her husband— that she put away her whoring from her face, and her adultery from between her breasts;

lest I strip her naked and make her as in the day she was born, and make her like a wilderness, and make her like a parched land, and kill her with thirst.

Upon her children also I will have no mercy, because they are children of whoredom.

For their mother has played the whore; she who conceived them has acted shamefully. For she said, 'I will go after my lovers, who give me my bread and my water, my wool and my flax, my oil and my drink.'

Therefore, I will hedge up her way with thorns, and I will build a wall against her, so that she cannot find her paths.

She shall pursue her lovers but not overtake them, and she shall seek them but shall not find them. Then she shall say, 'I will go and return to my first husband, for it was better for me then than now.'

And she did not know that it was I who gave her the grain, the wine, and the oil, and who lavished on her silver and gold, which they used for Baal.

Therefore, I will take back my grain in its time, and my wine in its season, and I will take away my wool and my flax, which were to cover her nakedness.
Now I will uncover her lewdness in the sight of her lovers, and no one shall rescue her out of my hand.
And I will put an end to all her mirth, her feasts, her new moons, her Sabbaths, and all her appointed feasts.
And I will lay waste her vines and her fig trees, of which she said, 'These are my wages, which my lovers have given me.' I will make them a forest, and the beasts of the field shall devour them.
And I will punish her for the feast days of the Baals when she burned offerings to them and adorned herself with her ring and jewelry, and went after her lovers and forgot me, declares the
LORD.
(Hos.2:1-3)

Let me break this passage down like this;

The marriage contract, or Ketubah, making process between God and Israel began with Abraham (Genesis 15:1-21, 17:1-27) and reached its culmination at Mount Sinai, where God gave Israel the Law (Exodus 19-24). However, Israel consistently failed to uphold their end of the covenant, engaging in spiritual adultery as described in Hosea 1-3.

Throughout the periods of the Judges (Judges 2:10-23, 8:33-34) and the monarchy (1 Kings 11:1-13, 14:21-31), Israel's idolatry and covenant disobedience led to cycles of judgment and restoration. Prophets like Isaiah, Jeremiah, and Ezekiel called Israel to repentance (Isaiah 1:2-4, Jeremiah 2:1-13, Ezekiel 16:1-63), but Israel's unfaithfulness persisted.

Under Roman rule, Herod's reign (37 BCE - 4 CE) marked a time of superficial religious revival. Many Jews attempted to reclaim their covenantal relationship with God through strict traditions and rituals (Matthew 3:1-12, Mark 12:1-12). Jesus' ministry occurred during this time, and He, like John the Baptist, preached a message of repentance and redemption (Matthew 4:17, Mark 1:14-15).

Israel's leaders, specifically the Levites, rejected Jesus as their Messiah, fulfilling prophecies like Psalm 118:22-23 and Isaiah 53:3. This rejection was symptomatic of a heart condition that had consistently led Israel to chase after other lovers (idols) instead of their faithful and loving husband (God).

Jesus' death on the cross marked the ultimate expression of God's love, but also signified Israel's final rejection of their Messiah and God the Father. Jesus lamented over Jerusalem's rejection, saying, "How often would I have gathered your children together as a hen gathers her brood under her wings, and you would not!" (Matthew 23:37).

Consequently, God rejected Israel as His wife, and the temple, a place of meeting and communion between God and His bride, was destroyed by the Roman army in 70 CE. This event formalized God's divorce from Israel (Hosea 2:2-13) and marked the end of the Mosaic Covenant.

However, Hosea 2:14-23 presents a surprising turn of events. Almost immediately after rejecting Israel as a wife under the old covenant, God speaks as a lover, wooing a shy and reluctant virgin to be His betrothed. This passage describes a future time when God will restore Israel and establish a new covenant with her, one that will be based on love, redemption, and faithfulness.

MYSTERY OF THE TWO COVENANTS

*"Therefore, behold, I will allure her, and bring her into the
wilderness, and speak tenderly to her.
And there I will give her her vineyards and make the Valley of
Achor a door of hope. And there she shall answer as in the days of
her youth, as at the time when she came out of the land of Egypt.
"And in that day, declares the LORD, you will call me 'My
Husband,' and no longer will you call me 'My Baal.'
For I will remove the names of the Baals from her mouth, and
they shall be remembered by name no more.
And I will make for them a covenant on that day with the beasts
of the field, the birds of the heavens, and the creeping things of
the ground. And I will abolish the bow, the sword, and war from
the land, and I will make you lie down in safety.
And I will betroth you to me forever. I will betroth you to me in
righteousness and in justice, in steadfast love and in mercy.
I will betroth you to me in faithfulness. And you shall know the
LORD.
"And in that day I will answer, declares the LORD, I will answer
the heavens, and they shall answer the earth,
and the earth shall answer the grain, the wine, and the oil, and
they shall answer Jezreel,
and I will sow her for myself in the land. And I will have mercy
on No Mercy, and I will say to Not My People, 'You are my
people'; and he shall say, 'You are my God.'"
(Hos.2:14-23)*

So, did God forsake Israel? No, He did not! While He did
divorce Israel as His wife under the Old Covenant, He did not
abandon her. In His love, mercy, and wisdom, God understood
Israel's heart condition, which the Old Covenant could not

address. The Old Covenant was never designed to transform the heart; it was meant to serve a specific purpose.

After the Old Covenant had fulfilled its purpose, which was to legally bring Jesus into the world, God brought it to a close. Two pivotal events marked the end of the Old Covenant era: the death of Jesus and the destruction of the temple.

The Death of Jesus

The first pivotal event was the death of Jesus. Even though God had divorced Israel, by Mosaic Law Israel was not free to marry another husband, that is Israel could not engage in another legally binding Ketubah until the first Ketubah expired. And the only way that was possible was if God the Husband died. God had to die, and he did that in the person of Jesus Christ.

The death of Jesus set the Israelites free to enter into a new covenant with a new husband. As the apostle Paul explained, "Do you not know, brothers—for I am speaking to those who know the law—that the law is binding on a person only as long as he lives?" (Romans 7:1). In other words, with Jesus' death, the Old Covenant was rendered obsolete, and a new covenant was established, one that would be based on faith, love, and the transformation of the heart.

For a married woman is bound by law to her husband while he lives, but if her husband dies she is released from the law of marriage.

Accordingly, she will be called an adulteress if she lives with another man while her husband is alive. But if her husband dies, she is free from that law, and if she marries another man she is not an adulteress.

Likewise, my brothers, you also have died to the law through the body of Christ, so that you may belong to another, to him who has been raised from the dead, in order that we may bear fruit for God.
For while we were living in the flesh, our sinful passions, aroused by the law, were at work in our members to bear fruit for death. But now we are released from the law, having died to that which held us captive, so that we serve in the new way of the Spirit and not in the old way of the written code.
(Rom 7:1-6)

Let me explain how the death of Jesus set Israel free from the Old covenant to marry yet again under a New Covenant.

"During His earthly ministry, Jesus perfectly represented the Father in every aspect. In fact, He embodied the Father's persona, agenda, and desires to such an extent that we can say He was on earth as the Father's divine representative. From His baptism onward, when the Father publicly acknowledged Him as 'My beloved Son, in whom I am well pleased' (Matthew 3:17), Jesus surrendered His own identity and will to fully align with the Father's.

Jesus perfectly embodied the Father's character and purpose. When Jesus spoke, it was the Father's voice; when He worked, it was the Father's power. During the Last Supper, Jesus communed with His disciples as the Father. Ultimately, Jesus' death on the cross actualized the sandal covenant, where He, as the Father's proxy, took responsibility for freeing humanity from the Old Covenant's requirements.

The Sandal Covenant tradition legally made Jesus Israel's husband here on earth, thus his death, fulfilled the Mosaic Law's requirements concerning Israel under the Old Covenant.

This set Israel free to engage with God on a new basis – a new marriage covenant.

The sandal covenant between God the Father and Jesus is pivotal to understanding Paul's argument in Romans 7. Paul explained that the Romans were no longer bound by the Old Covenant because, from that covenant's perspective, their husband (God the Father) had died. This death liberated them to enter into a new covenant with Jesus.

To alleviate their fear of breaking covenant and its consequences, the writer of Hebrews addressed the changing of the priesthood. By exploring this concept, we gain a deeper understanding of the transition from the Old Covenant to the New Covenant, and the implications this has for our relationship with God.

For when there is a change in the priesthood, there is necessarily a change in the law as well.

For the one of whom these things are spoken belonged to another tribe, from which no one has ever served at the altar.

For it is evident that our Lord was descended from Judah, and in connection with that tribe Moses said nothing about priests.

This becomes even more evident when another priest arises in the likeness of Melchizedek,

who has become a priest, not on the basis of a legal requirement concerning bodily descent, but by the power of an indestructible life.

For it is witnessed of him, "You are a priest forever, after the order of Melchizedek.

(Heb. 7:12-17)

The dual significance of the death of Jesus

Before we move on to the second pivotal event, I want to address something briefly.

Jesus' death held a dual significance. On one hand, He bore the weight of humanity's sins, becoming sin itself, so that we might become the righteousness of God. This sacrifice paid our sin debt, fulfilling the curse of Deuteronomy 21:23. As the groom of the Church, Jesus' death was the ultimate act of love, securing our redemption and freedom from the mastery of sin.

On the other hand, Jesus' death also represented the culmination of His role as Israel's husband. By dying, Jesus set Israel free from the obligations and constraints of the Old Covenant. This liberation allowed Israel to be free to marry Jesus again, but this time under a new covenant. This new covenant was sealed with Jesus' blood, which was shed as the bride price to redeem Israel and secure her as His bride.

We have already learnt that in ancient Jewish tradition, the bride price was a payment made by the groom to the bride's family to secure her hand in marriage. In this context, Jesus' blood was the ultimate bride price, paid to redeem Israel and secure her as His beloved. This profound act of love and sacrifice not only demonstrated Jesus' commitment to Israel but also underscored the depth of His love for humanity.

So, through His death, Jesus achieved two remarkable goals. He freed Israel from the Old Covenant, allowing her to enter into a new and more intimate relationship with Him. Simultaneously, He redeemed humanity from the mastery of sin, offering us a new covenant based on faith, love, and the transformation of the heart. Jesus' death was a singular event that held multiple significance, speaking to the complexity and richness of God's plan for humanity.

The significance of the Destruction of the Temple

Now that I have that out of the way let's move onto the second pivotal event was the Destruction of the Temple, Because the Levitical priesthood, performed the duties of Gods bride in Gods Ketubah with Israel, there is no way that he could set aside the old covenant without setting aside the Levitical priesthood. And because the priesthood could not function without the temple when he made sure that the temple was destroyed by the Romans. Personally I believe that God has allowed an alternative religion (Islam) to rise up and contest the Israelites for the very site on which the temple had stood on order to stop Israel from rebuilding the temple and reinstituting the service of the Levitical priesthood.

Jeremiah foretold:

"Behold, the days are coming...when I will make a new covenant with the house of Israel and the house of Judah...not according to the covenant that I made with their fathers" (Jeremiah 31:31-34).

We have already learned that in traditional Jewish marriage, each stage of Kiddushin—the calling, sanctification, and betrothal—progressively deepens the covenant between the groom and bride, marked by symbolic cups of wine that represent commitment and promise. Jesus' ministry among His disciples reflects these covenantal steps, symbolically leading them, and by extension all of Israel, into a New Covenant that culminates in a renewed, eternal union with God. Each key moment in Jesus' ministry takes on profound covenantal meaning, weaving together the fulfillment of Old Testament promises with the institution of the New Covenant.

1. **The Covenant of Servanthood: The Calling and Setting Apart of the Disciples**

   The first stage of Kiddushin, the calling and setting apart of the bride, is reflected in Jesus' calling of the twelve disciples. This act of sanctification, represented by the initial Cup of Sanctification in the Kiddushin tradition, sets the disciples apart as Jesus' own representatives and covenant people. Through His choice, Jesus calls each disciple individually, inviting them to follow Him and setting them apart for a unique purpose (Matthew 4:18-22).

This act of setting apart is reminiscent of the initial covenant established between God and Israel at Sinai, where Israel was sanctified as God's treasured possession (Exodus 19:5-6). Similarly, Jesus sets apart the disciples as symbolic "fathers" of a new covenant people, embodying a spiritual Israel that will carry forth God's kingdom message. By doing so, Jesus establishes a new covenantal relationship with His disciples, one that will be further deepened and fulfilled through the subsequent stages of the Kiddushin process.

1. **The Salt Covenant of friendship and Hospitality: Jesus' Commissioning and Sending of the Disciples**

The second stage of Kiddushin, the salt covenant of friendship and hospitality, is seen in Jesus' commissioning and sending of the disciples. As part of this process, Jesus grants them authority to preach the kingdom of God and perform signs, consecrating them as covenant emissaries. This act of commissioning, as recorded in Luke 9:1-2, represents a deepening of commitment within the Kiddushin framework, paralleling the groom's pledge to protect and provide for his bride.

This moment marks a significant milestone in the disciples' journey, as they are empowered to declare the coming kingdom and perform signs. Jesus' granting of authority serves as a tangible expression of His commitment to His disciples, demonstrating His intention to provide for and protect them as their bridegroom.

The first cup of wine shared at the Last Supper symbolizes the first covenantal commitment of the groom, marking the disciples' formal entrance into the New Covenant with Jesus as the bridegroom. Furthermore, Jesus' washing of the disciples' feet reflects the sandal covenant of inheritance, representing the groom's pledge to provide for his bride. This act of humility and service prepares the disciples for their role as Jesus' covenantal partners, demonstrating His commitment to care for and provide for them.

MYSTERY OF THE TWO COVENANTS

1. **The First Cup at the Last Supper: Commitment in the Betrothal**

    The Last Supper serves as the official betrothal meal, symbolizing the disciples' formal entrance into the New Covenant with Jesus as the bridegroom. During this meal, Jesus shares the first of two cups of wine with the disciples, saying, "Take this and divide it among yourselves. For I tell you that from now on I will not drink of the fruit of the vine until the kingdom of God comes" (Luke 22:17-18). This initial cup, shared before the meal, symbolizes the first covenantal commitment of the groom, marking the disciples as those entering into the Kiddushin. By sharing this cup, Jesus formally initiates the betrothal process, committing Himself to the disciples as their bridegroom and welcoming them into the New Covenant.

1. **The Sandal Covenant of Inheritance: The Washing of the Disciples' Feet**

    Jesus' washing of the disciples' feet, as recorded in John 13, reflects the sandal covenant of inheritance, which represents the groom's pledge to provide for his bride. This act of humility and service, rooted in Jewish cultural traditions of hospitality, cleansing, and humility, prepares the disciples for their role as Jesus' covenantal partners.

By performing this act, Jesus not only sanctifies His disciples for the mission but also exemplifies the servant-hearted nature of His bride. His words, "If I do not wash you, you have no share with me" (John 13:8), underscore this washing as a symbolic cleansing, preparing the disciples as His covenantal partners. This act of purification reflects the consecration required to enter into a divine relationship, demonstrating Jesus' commitment to provide for and care for His bride.

1. **The Second Cup at the Last Supper: The Cup of the New Covenant**

   After the meal, Jesus shares a second cup of wine, declaring, "This cup is the new covenant in my blood, which is poured out for you" (Luke 22:20). This second cup represents the Cup of the New Covenant, sealing the betrothal with His sacrificial blood, which will be shed on the cross. By doing so, Jesus fulfills the covenantal requirements on behalf of His people, paying the ultimate bride price to secure His bride. This act signifies the completion of the betrothal, an irrevocable commitment that binds Jesus to His bride—the people of the New Covenant.

This moment inaugurates the New Covenant prophesied by Jeremiah, where God will "write His law on their hearts" (Jeremiah 31:33), bringing His people into intimate, heart-deep union with Himself. As Jesus invites the disciples to drink from this cup, He welcomes them into this new covenantal relationship, one that will be marked by a deepening of commitment, love, and devotion.

1. **The Cup of Redemption: The Wine-Vinegar on the Cross**

   As Jesus hangs on the cross, He is offered a cup of sour wine, or vinegar, which He drinks (John 19:28-30). This cup fulfills the Cup of Redemption, symbolizing both His suffering and the culmination of His covenantal journey. In the context of Kiddushin, the Cup of Redemption often corresponds to a pledge of inheritance or assurance that the groom will return. By accepting the sour wine, Jesus completes the Kiddushin process, affirming the redemption He has secured for His bride and declaring, "It is finished." This final act of love seals the New Covenant, establishing the bride's inheritance and awaiting the consummation at the final wedding feast.

1. **The Great Commission: Sending Forth His Betrothed as Witnesses of the Covenant**

   After His resurrection, Jesus gives the disciples the Great Commission (Matthew 28:18-20), sending them into the world as His covenantal representatives. This commissioning acts as the formal sending of the bride to prepare for the coming kingdom, where she will be united with her bridegroom. With this mandate, Jesus grants the disciples all the authority He had been given, invoking the sandal covenant and entrusting them to represent Him on earth.

The promise that He will be with them until the end of the age serves as His assurance that He will enforce their exercise of His authority. Empowered by this authority, the disciples are sent to make disciples of all nations, carrying the covenant promises forward and inviting others to join in the New Covenant community. This mission represents the bride's ongoing preparation, spreading the covenant love of God to all nations in anticipation of the final union.

1. The Final Cup of Consummation: The Wedding Supper of the Lamb

The ultimate Cup of Consummation, or Cup of Praise, will be shared in the future, as described in Revelation 19:7-9 at the Wedding Supper of the Lamb. Here, Jesus' covenant with His bride will be fully consummated, bringing to fulfillment His words at the Last Supper: "I tell you, I will not drink from this fruit of the vine from now on until that day when I drink it new with you in my Father's kingdom" (Matthew 26:29). This future feast marks the completion of the covenantal journey, where all who belong to Christ, having been redeemed and prepared, will be united with Him in eternal joy.

At the Wedding Supper of the Lamb, Jesus' sacrificial love and the promises of the New Covenant are celebrated in full. This Final Cup represents the everlasting union between Jesus and His bride, bound in a love that was sealed by His own blood. No longer is it just a promise or foretaste; this final cup signifies the consummated relationship between God and

His people, a bond of unending intimacy, joy, and divine fulfillment.

Just as a groom and bride rejoice on their wedding day, the coming kingdom will reveal the ultimate fulfillment of God's promises. The Cup of Consummation is not merely an end but the beginning of an eternal union, a relationship perfected through Jesus' sacrifice and the hope of His return, when the bride will drink anew with the Bridegroom in His Father's kingdom. Here, the joy and praise of the union will resonate eternally, completing the divine plan that began with a covenant invitation and culminates in the everlasting joy of communion with God.

9. The Final Cup of Praise: The Wedding Supper of the Lamb

The ultimate "Cup of Praise" will be shared in the future, as Revelation 19:7-9 describes the Wedding Supper of the Lamb. Here, Jesus' covenant with His bride will be fully consummated, fulfilling His words at the Last Supper that He would "drink it new with you in my Father's kingdom" (Matthew 26:29). This final cup signifies the everlasting joy of the union between Jesus and His bride, a relationship bound by His sacrificial love and the New Covenant promises.

Through each of these covenantal moments—calling, sanctifying, sending, and ultimately redeeming—Jesus symbolically fulfills the Kiddushin covenant. His ministry becomes a divine betrothal process, preparing His disciples as representatives of the bride who will one day celebrate eternal union with the bridegroom. In these events, we see the foundation of a relationship with God not just as a follower or a servant, but as a beloved bride—forever united in the promise of His love.

Conclusion

As we conclude this chapter, we've journeyed through the prophetic messages that foreshadowed a New Covenant—a covenant that would transcend the old legal frameworks and open a pathway to an intimate, transformative relationship with God through Christ. The Old Covenant, represented by the law given to Israel, was essential in preparing the way for Christ. Yet, as we've seen, this covenant ultimately pointed beyond itself, revealing its limitations and the need for a more profound heart transformation that only the New Covenant could fulfill.

Jesus introduced a radically different paradigm that would not only redefine but also fulfill the law's deeper spiritual intentions. His ministry established a new covenantal framework—a framework where faith and relationship supersede ritual and regulation, and where love and grace form the cornerstone of God's relationship with His people. Jesus' role as the Bridegroom represents a renewed covenant that, unlike the old, speaks to both Jew and Gentile, inviting all into a unified body—the Church. This New Covenant, unlike the Mosaic Covenant, is not one of conditional blessings based on adherence to the law but of unconditional grace, realized through Christ's atoning sacrifice.

Chapter 9: The Atonement and Salvation in the New Covenant; Jesus the Bridegroom and the Church as His Bride

Introduction

The New Covenant, as revealed through Christ's life, death, and resurrection, represents a transformative shift in how humanity relates to God. This chapter builds upon the theological foundation laid in Chapter 8, emphasizing the covenantal dynamics between Jesus as the Bridegroom and the Church as His Bride. By examining the atonement and salvation within this covenantal framework, we will explore how Christ fulfilled the Mosaic Law, secured redemption, and established a new relational paradigm. Additionally, we will address how this view harmonizes with the traditional doctrines of salvation and atonement, highlighting its implications for both individual believers and the Church as a whole.

As we journey through this chapter, we will explore several key theological concepts: the role of Jesus as the Bridegroom, the fulfillment of the Mosaic Law, the covenantal implications for the Church, and the relationship between the New Covenant and the coming Kingdom. These themes will converge to illuminate the depth of Christ's work and its transformative power for His Bride, the Church.

Jesus the Bridegroom: Fulfilling the Law and

Establishing the New Covenant

The Bridegroom Metaphor in Scripture

Throughout His ministry, Jesus referred to Himself as the Bridegroom, drawing upon rich prophetic imagery. John the Baptist affirmed this identity, declaring, "The friend of the bridegroom, who stands and hears him, rejoices greatly at the bridegroom's voice" (John 3:29). This metaphor connects to Hosea's depiction of God as a husband longing to restore an unfaithful bride (Hosea 2:14-23). In the New Covenant, Jesus fulfills this imagery, representing a groom who secures His bride through sacrificial love (Ephesians 5:25-27).

This metaphor carries profound covenantal implications. Unlike the Mosaic Covenant, which bound God and Israel through a conditional legal agreement, the New Covenant offers unconditional grace, reflecting the enduring faithfulness of a bridegroom to his bride. Jesus' use of this imagery not only affirms His messianic identity but also redefines the covenantal relationship between God and humanity, extending it to include all who believe in Him.

Fulfilling the Mosaic Law

The New Covenant did not abolish the Old Covenant but fulfilled its requirements. Jesus lived a sinless life, embodying perfect obedience to the Mosaic Law. His death satisfied its demands for atonement (Leviticus 17:11, Romans 8:3-4), and His resurrection proved His acceptance by the Father (Romans 4:25). In doing so, He became the unblemished Lamb of God, whose sacrifice covers sin once and for all (Hebrews 9:11-14).

By fulfilling the Law, Jesus secured His position as the perfect Bridegroom, capable of mediating a new and eternal covenant with His Bride, the Church. This fulfillment ensured that the Mosaic Covenant could transition into the New Covenant without violating God's holiness or justice.

The Mosaic Covenant was contractual, rooted in blessings and curses contingent upon obedience (Deuteronomy 28). The New Covenant, however, is unconditional, rooted in grace and sealed by Christ's blood (Luke 22:20). By fulfilling the Old Covenant, Jesus paved the way for a relationship not based on human effort but on divine love and mercy.

The Role of the Bridegroom in Covenant Mediation

As the Bridegroom, Jesus not only fulfills the Law but also mediates the New Covenant on behalf of His bride. This union is central to the Church's relationship with God. Paul writes, "For through Him we both have access in one Spirit to the Father" (Ephesians 2:18). Through Christ, believers are presented as righteous before the Father, not by their merit, but by their union with the Bridegroom.

The Church as the Bride of Christ: Salvation through Union with the Bridegroom

Formation of the New Covenant Community

The Church is more than a collection of individuals; it is the Bride of Christ, united through His covenantal sacrifice. This relationship is communal and relational, reflecting the unity of a bride with her groom. Paul uses marriage as a metaphor to describe this spiritual union: "This mystery is profound, and I am saying that it refers to Christ and the church" (Ephesians 5:32).

Blood Covenant of Servanthood

The Blood Covenant of Servanthood represented by the first cup at the Last Supper (Luke 22:17), this cup symbolizes the sanctification of the bride. Through the shedding of His blood, Jesus cleansed the Church, setting it apart for Himself.

The Salt Covenant of Friendship and Dedication

The breaking of bread at the Last Supper signifies a covenant of dedication, where Jesus offers Himself as the provision for His bride (Luke 22:19).

The Sandal Covenant of Redemption

The sour wine offered to Jesus on the cross (John 19:28-30) represents the price of redemption, sealing the inheritance of the Church as co-heirs with Christ (Romans 8:17).

The Bride's Acceptance through the Groom

As members of the Church, believers are accepted by the Father not on their own merit but through their covenantal union with Christ. This aligns with the ancient Hebraic marriage tradition, where the bride's standing was secured by her relationship with the groom. Jesus' declaration, "I am the way, and the truth, and the life. No one comes to the Father except through me" (John 14:6), underscores this covenantal dynamic.

The Inclusion of the Gentiles: A Unified Covenant Community

Unification of Jew and Gentile

The New Covenant, established through Jesus Christ, extends God's promises beyond the borders of Israel, embracing people from all nations. This development fulfills the prophecy of Isaiah, who foretold that God's people would become "a light for the nations, that my salvation may reach to the end of the earth" (Isaiah 49:6). Through Christ, Gentiles are welcomed into the covenant community, being grafted into the olive tree of God's people, as explained by Paul in Romans 11:17-24.

Paul's vision emphasizes the unity of Jew and Gentile within the New Covenant. He writes, "For in one Spirit we were all baptized into one body—Jews or Greeks, slaves or free—and all were made to drink of one Spirit" (1 Corinthians 12:13). This unified body, comprised of people from diverse backgrounds, reflects the communal nature of the bride, bound together by the Spirit in preparation for the Bridegroom's return.

In this sense, the New Covenant community is a preview of the ultimate wedding feast, where people from every nation will gather to celebrate the union of Christ and His bride. The Spirit's work in uniting believers across cultural and ethnic lines foreshadows the ultimate reconciliation that will occur when Christ returns to claim His bride.

The Fulfillment and Future of the Marriage Covenant

Awaiting the Consummation

The covenantal journey of the Church will culminate in the Marriage Supper of the Lamb, as described in Revelation 19:7-9. This future event represents the consummation of the bride's union with Christ, fulfilling His promise to "drink it new with you in my Father's kingdom" (Matthew 26:29).

Eschatological Implications

The bridal identity of the Church points to its role in the coming Kingdom. As Daniel foretold, the Son of Man will establish an everlasting dominion (Daniel 7:13-14). The Church, as the bride, will reign with Christ, reflecting His glory and participating in His Eternal Kingdom (Revelation 22:5).

Living Out the New Covenant Today

Implications for Believers

Living as the Bride of Christ calls for a life of holiness, love, and service. As Paul exhorts, "Walk in a manner worthy of the calling to which you have been called" (Ephesians 4:1). This includes embodying the values of the New Covenant, reflecting God's grace and love to the world.

Communal and Individual Responsibility

The Church, as a covenant community, is called to demonstrate the unity and love of Christ. This involves both personal transformation and collective mission, as Paul describes in Romans 12:1-8.

Conclusion

The New Covenant, secured through Jesus' life, death, and resurrection, redefines humanity's relationship with God. As the Bridegroom, Jesus fulfills the Law and establishes a relationship of unconditional grace with His Church, His bride. This covenant invites believers into a communal and eternal union with God, culminating in the Marriage Supper of the Lamb.

As we move into the next chapter, we will explore how this New Covenant paradigm shapes the daily life and faith of believers, addressing the apparent tensions between the New Covenant and the Mosaic Law while revealing the transformative power of grace in Christ.

Chapter 10: The Standard of Righteousness in the New Covenant: The Bride's Call to Intimacy and Restoration

Introduction

The journey from the Old Covenant, established between God the Father and Israel, to the New Covenant, mediated through Jesus Christ and His Bride, the Church, represents not merely a shift in legal frameworks but a profound reimagining of righteousness and relationship. At the heart of this transition lies God's ultimate desire: to restore humanity's broken heart condition, heal the alienation wrought by sin, and draw His family of sons and daughters into eternal communion with Himself. This chapter explores the unique standard of righteousness that defines the New Covenant, its expectations for the Bride of Christ, and its role in fulfilling God's redemptive plan.

The Old Covenant: A Standard of Righteousness Rooted in the Mosaic Law

The Mosaic Covenant was a marriage contract (Ketubah) between God the Father and Israel, His chosen bride. As outlined in Exodus 19-24, this covenant was built upon laws and statutes that delineated the terms of this union. These laws, summarized in the Ten Commandments

and expanded upon in the Torah, served as a divine framework for holiness, justice, and worship. They reflected God's immutable character and established Israel's identity as His people.

Under the Old Covenant, righteousness was defined by adherence to the Law. God's blessings were conditional upon Israel's obedience, as seen in Deuteronomy 28, where both blessings for compliance and curses for disobedience are detailed. However, this framework revealed humanity's inability to fulfill God's standards due to the hardness of the human heart (Jeremiah 17:9). Despite its divine origins, the Mosaic Law served as a "tutor" to point humanity to the need for a Savior (Galatians 3:24).

The New Covenant: A Higher Calling Rooted in Grace

In the New Covenant, the relationship shifts from a contractual agreement with Israel to a relational union between Jesus, the Father's firstborn Son, and His Bride, the Church. Just as the Mosaic Covenant defined Israel's identity and expectations, the New Covenant introduces a new standard of righteousness tailored to this divine union.

This standard, while no longer tied to the letter of the Mosaic Law, is not antithetical to it. Jesus stated, "Do not think that I have come to abolish the Law or the Prophets; I have not come to abolish them but to fulfill them" (Matthew 5:17). In fulfilling the Law, Jesus satisfied its demands, embodying its principles in a way that transcended mere legal adherence and introduced a higher, heart-centered standard.

The New Covenant's Standard of Righteousness:

Faith and Love

Under the New Covenant, righteousness is no longer achieved through works of the Law but through faith in Christ. Paul writes, "For Christ is the end of the law for righteousness to everyone who believes" (Romans 10:4). This righteousness is imputed to believers based on their union with Christ, the perfect Bridegroom, who fulfilled all the requirements of the Law on their behalf.

This does not mean the New Covenant is without expectations. Rather, its expectations flow from a transformed heart. The essence of the New Covenant is summarized in Jeremiah 31:33: "I will put my law within them, and I will write it on their hearts. And I will be their God, and they shall be my people."

Jesus introduced a new commandment to His disciples: "A new commandment I give to you, that you love one another: just as I have loved you, you also are to love one another" (John 13:34). Love, rather than legal compliance, becomes the defining mark of righteousness in the New Covenant. This love fulfills the deeper intention of the Law: "For the whole law is fulfilled in one word: 'You shall love your neighbor as yourself'" (Galatians 5:14).

While the New Covenant emphasizes grace, it also calls the Bride to a life of holiness and faithfulness. Paul exhorts believers, "Present your bodies as a living sacrifice, holy and acceptable to God, which is your spiritual worship" (Romans 12:1). The Bride's righteousness is not about rule-keeping but about reflecting the character of her Bridegroom through love, humility, and service.

The New Covenant as a Divine "Cheat Code"

The New Covenant can be likened to a divine "cheat code" built into the redemptive story. While the Mosaic Law reveals the impossibility of achieving righteousness through human effort, the New Covenant provides a solution: righteousness by grace through faith. This "cheat code" does not nullify the Law but fulfills it, offering believers the benefits of covenantal blessings without the penalties of covenantal curses.

Paul captures this beautifully: "For by grace you have been saved through faith. And this is not your own doing; it is the gift of God, not a result of works, so that no one may boast" (Ephesians 2:8-9). This grace empowers believers to live according to the Spirit, producing the fruit of righteousness (Galatians 5:22-23).

The overarching purpose of both the Old and New Covenants is to restore humanity's broken relationship with God. The Law exposed humanity's sinfulness, while the New Covenant offers the solution: a heart transformation through the Holy Spirit. Ezekiel prophesied this transformation: "I will give you a new heart, and a new spirit I will put within you" (Ezekiel 36:26).

God's ultimate goal is to bring humanity back to its original state in the Garden of Eden—a state of unbroken communion and intimacy with Him. Revelation 21:3 describes this fulfillment: "Behold, the dwelling place of God is with man. He will dwell with them, and they will be His people, and God Himself will be with them as their God." The New Covenant is the means by which God achieves this vision, preparing a Bride who is ready to dwell with Him forever.

The Role of the Bride in the New Covenant

A Call to Intimacy

The Bride of Christ is called to a life of intimacy with her Bridegroom. This intimacy is cultivated through worship, prayer, and obedience to the Spirit's leading. The Church's relationship with Christ is not merely positional but deeply relational, reflecting the union of a bride with her groom.

A Call to Mission

As the Bride, the Church is also called to participate in God's mission to reconcile the world to Himself. Paul describes believers as "ambassadors for Christ" (2 Corinthians 5:20), entrusted with the message of reconciliation. This mission reflects God's desire for all humanity to be restored to Him.

7. Harmonizing the Old and New Covenants

The New Covenant does not negate the Old Covenant but fulfills its ultimate purpose. The Mosaic Law remains a picture of God's immutable standards, revealing His holiness and justice. However, under the New Covenant, believers are judged not by the letter of the Law but by their union with Christ, who perfectly fulfilled it.

Jesus' teaching in the Sermon on the Mount exemplifies the higher standard of the New Covenant. Rather than merely prohibiting external actions like murder or adultery, Jesus addresses the heart condition that leads to sin (Matthew 5:21-30). This higher standard underscores the transformative nature of the New Covenant, which empowers believers to live out God's righteousness from the inside out.

Conclusion

The New Covenant establishes a standard of righteousness that transcends legalistic rule-keeping, calling believers into a life of love, faith, and holiness. Through their union with Christ, the Bridegroom, the Church is empowered to fulfill God's ultimate desire: a family of sons and daughters who live in intimate communion with Him.

This covenantal relationship not only restores humanity to its original purpose but also equips the Bride to reflect God's glory and participate in His mission of reconciliation. As we move forward, we will explore how the Church, as the Bride of Christ, interacts with the coming Kingdom, fulfilling its role in God's eternal plan.

Chapter 11: The Church and the Kingdom of God: A Royal Priesthood in the Order of Melchizedek

The Church and the Kingdom of God, while deeply interconnected, remain distinct within the divine framework of God's redemptive plan. The Kingdom of God encompasses His eternal rule, manifesting His justice, love, and sovereignty over all creation. The Church, on the other hand, represents the *ekklesia*—a community called out to embody God's will and serve as His emissary on earth. To fully grasp the Church's role as the reborn Melchizedek priesthood within this Kingdom, it is vital to explore its theological roots in Israel's Levitical priesthood, its transformation through Jesus Christ, and its ultimate purpose in God's cosmic design.

The Kingdom of God: Sovereign and Eternal

The Kingdom of God represents the ultimate expression of God's sovereignty. From eternity past, God has reigned as Creator and King over all creation, governing the seen and unseen realms. His Kingdom is eternal, transcending time and space, as declared by the psalmist: "Your kingdom is an everlasting kingdom, and your dominion endures through all generations" (Psalm 145:13).

In the ministry of Jesus, the Kingdom of God was revealed as both a present reality and a future hope. Jesus' proclamation, "The Kingdom of God is at hand" (Mark 1:15), signaled the arrival of a spiritual reign inaugurated through His presence. Yet, the fullness of this Kingdom awaits the eschatological culmination described in Revelation, where the Kingdoms of this world become the Kingdom of our Lord and of His Christ (Revelation 11:15).

This dual nature of the Kingdom—already here but not yet fully realized—forms the foundation of its interaction with the Church. While the Kingdom encompasses God's sovereign rule over all, the Church is the visible and tangible instrument through which His will is enacted on earth.

The Church as Ecclesia: A Called-Out Assembly

The Greek term *ekklesia*, meaning "called-out assembly," offers profound insight into the Church's identity and purpose. In ancient Greece, an *ekklesia* referred to a legislative assembly of citizens called to deliberate and enact the will of the state. Similarly, the Church is called out from the world to deliberate and enact the will of God, serving as His ambassadors and reflecting His Kingdom on earth.

The Church exists as a covenantal community bound by the New Covenant established in Christ's blood. Its members are not merely individuals who believe but a collective Bride united with the Bridegroom, Jesus Christ. Peter's description of the Church as a "royal priesthood" (1 Peter 2:9) underscores this dual role: the Church is both a spiritual community of priests and a royal entity tasked with advancing the Kingdom's values.

While the Kingdom of God is universal and eternal, the Church functions as its earthly agent, tasked with manifesting the Kingdom's principles in a fallen world. Through its mission of worship, discipleship, and service, the Church bridges the gap between the divine and the temporal, embodying the Kingdom's transformative power.

The Church as the Reborn Melchizedek Priesthood

The concept of the Church as a priesthood takes its ultimate form in the Order of Melchizedek—a priesthood that predates and surpasses the Levitical system. To understand this role, we must first consider the function of the Levitical priesthood in the Old Covenant and how it foreshadowed a greater, eternal priesthood to come.

The Levitical Priesthood: A Foreshadowing

Under the Mosaic Covenant, the Levitical priesthood served as mediators between God and Israel. Chosen from the tribe of Levi, these priests performed sacred duties, offering sacrifices, teaching the Law, and maintaining the sanctity of the tabernacle (Numbers 3:5-10; Deuteronomy 33:8-10). Their role was essential in preserving Israel's covenantal relationship with God, ensuring that the people remained consecrated to Him.

God's original intention for Israel was to function as a nation of priests, a holy people reflecting His character to the nations (Exodus 19:6). However, following the sin of the golden calf, this role was restricted to the Levites, who became the exclusive mediators of God's holiness.

For a time, the Levitical priesthood, alongside prophets and judges, provided spiritual and civil leadership under God's direct rule. However, when Israel demanded a king to rule over them, rejecting God as their sovereign, the priesthood's role within the Kingdom was diminished (1 Samuel 8:4-7). This transition marked a departure from God's ideal theocracy, where the priesthood would have served as the Bride mediating His rule.

Jesus and the Order of Melchizedek

The Levitical priesthood, while divinely instituted, was always meant to be provisional, pointing toward a superior priesthood. The Order of Melchizedek, first introduced in Genesis 14:18-20, embodies this greater reality. Melchizedek, the king-priest of Salem, blessed Abraham and received his tithe, symbolizing a priesthood that transcends ethnicity, lineage, and time.

Psalm 110:4 prophesied the coming of a Messiah who would be "a priest forever in the order of Melchizedek," a prophecy fulfilled in Jesus Christ. The writer of Hebrews expounds on this, emphasizing Jesus' eternal priesthood:

- Unlike the Levitical priests, Jesus serves forever, based on the power of an indestructible life (Hebrews 7:16).
- His priesthood is universal, encompassing all nations and peoples (Hebrews 7:2-3).
- He offered Himself as the ultimate sacrifice, rendering the Levitical system obsolete (Hebrews 9:11-14).

Through His death and resurrection, Jesus inaugurates the New Covenant and establishes the Church as His Bride and as the inheritor of the Melchizedekian mantle.

The Church as a Royal Priesthood

The Church's identity as a royal priesthood signifies its participation in both priestly and kingly functions. This dual role reflects the nature of Melchizedek, who was both king of Salem and priest of God Most High.

Priestly Functions

As a priestly community, the Church mediates between God and the world, fulfilling the following roles:

- **Intercession**: Just as the Levitical priests interceded for Israel, the Church is called to pray for all people, standing in the gap for a broken world (1 Timothy 2:1-5).
- **Sacrificial Living**: Believers are urged to offer their bodies as living sacrifices, holy and pleasing to God, embodying a life of worship (Romans 12:1).
- **Proclamation**: The Church is tasked with proclaiming the gospel, bringing the message of reconciliation to the ends of the earth (Matthew 28:19-20).

Royal Functions

As a royal entity, the Church reflects the authority and glory of Christ's Kingdom. Believers are co-heirs with Christ, destined to reign with Him in the coming Kingdom (Romans 8:17; Revelation 22:5). The Church advances the Kingdom by living out its values of justice, mercy, and love, serving as a light in a dark world (Matthew 5:13-16).

The Church and the Kingdom: A Divine

Partnership

The Church interacts with the Kingdom of God as its representative and instrument. While the Kingdom encompasses God's universal reign, the Church serves as its earthly embassy, embodying its principles and advancing its mission.

The Church fulfills its role by:

- **Making Disciples**: Equipping believers to grow in faith and reflect Kingdom values.
- **Evangelizing the Lost**: Extending the invitation to join the covenant community.
- **Demonstrating Justice and Mercy**: Addressing social injustices and caring for the marginalized as a reflection of Kingdom ethics.

The Church's ultimate purpose is to prepare for the eschatological fulfillment of the Kingdom, when Christ will return to reign in glory and the Church will be united with Him as His Bride at the Wedding Supper of the Lamb (Revelation 19:7-9).

The Two Marriage Covenants and the Priesthoods

The First Covenant: God the Father and Israel (The Mosaic Marriage Covenant)

In the first covenant, the marriage framework presents God the Father as the bridegroom of Israel. This covenant, enacted through the Mosaic Law, was mediated by the Levitical priesthood, which served as the bride (the intermediary) within the theocratic Kingdom of Israel. The Levites were set apart to teach the Law, offer sacrifices, and maintain covenant fidelity on behalf of Israel.

This priesthood played a central role in sustaining the Mosaic covenant, functioning as a relational bridge between God and His people. However, the framework of this covenant was based on conditional blessings and curses (Deuteronomy 28), and it failed to address humanity's deeper heart condition. Israel's unfaithfulness, exemplified by idolatry and disobedience, revealed the limitations of the Levitical priesthood and the need for a superior covenantal structure.

As part of this failure, the people demanded a human king, rejecting God as their sole ruler (1 Samuel 8:4-7). This marked a departure from God's original design of a priestly nation, where He alone was the King, and His covenant bride functioned as His representative on earth.

The New Covenant shifts the focus to a different relational dynamic. In this framework, Jesus, the Son and firstborn of the Father, becomes the bridegroom, entering into covenantal relationship with the Church. This covenant, unlike the

Mosaic one, is founded on grace and faith rather than adherence to the Law.

Here, the priesthood is no longer Levitical but Melchizedekian. Jesus, as the eternal High Priest in the order of Melchizedek, mediates the covenant. His role transcends lineage, ethnicity, and geography, reflecting the universal scope of the New Covenant (Hebrews 7:11-28).

Through this covenant, the Church inherits the mantle of priesthood, becoming a "royal priesthood" (1 Peter 2:9). As the Bride of Christ, the Church carries forward the priestly responsibilities of intercession, proclamation, and worship, mirroring and fulfilling the role originally envisioned for Israel.

The Levitical priesthood, tied to the Mosaic covenant, was inherently temporary, designed to point toward the coming of a superior priesthood. This transition is beautifully encapsulated in Hebrews 8:6, which declares:

"But as it is, Christ has obtained a ministry that is as much more excellent than the old as the covenant He mediates is better, since it is enacted on better promises."

This transition marks the shift from the old covenant's reliance on external law to the new covenant's focus on internal transformation. The Levitical priesthood, dependent on legalistic rituals, gave way to the Melchizedekian priesthood, which operates through the indestructible life and eternal priesthood of Christ (Hebrews 7:16).

Under the New Covenant, the Church does not operate under the Mosaic Law but fulfills its deeper purposes. This is what Paul explains in Romans 8:2-4:

"For the law of the Spirit of life has set you free in Christ Jesus from the law of sin and death. For God has done what the law, weakened by the flesh, could not do."

The Church's priestly role under the New Covenant aligns with the Melchizedekian framework, emphasizing grace, Spirit-empowerment, and relational intimacy with God.

The Church's role as Bride is inherently priestly. In the ancient Hebrew context, the bride shared in the husband's responsibilities and mission. For the Church, this means partnering with Christ to mediate God's presence to the world, reflecting the original priestly call given to humanity in Eden.

Where Israel failed to fully embody its calling as a nation of priests (Exodus 19:6), the Church fulfills this role under the New Covenant. The Church's royal priesthood is empowered by the indwelling Holy Spirit, enabling believers to serve as both intercessors and representatives of God's Kingdom on earth.

Through this priesthood, the Church advances the Kingdom, proclaiming the gospel, discipling nations, and demonstrating the values of God's reign. This fulfills God's ultimate plan to restore humanity to its original state of communion with Him, as exemplified in the Garden of Eden.

The Eschatological Union: The Church as the Bride of Christ

The two marriage covenants culminate in the eschatological vision of Revelation. The Mosaic covenant, with its limitations, served to prepare the way for the New Covenant, where the Church is presented as the spotless Bride of Christ (Ephesians 5:25-27; Revelation 19:7-9).

This union completes God's redemptive plan:

1. **A Restored Family of Priests**: The Church becomes the royal priesthood God always intended, mediating His presence in a redeemed creation.
2. **The Consummation of the Kingdom**: At the Wedding Supper of the Lamb, the Church and the Kingdom of God converge, marking the eternal reign of Christ and His Bride (Revelation 21:1-4).

Conclusion: A Unified Narrative

The two marriage covenants and the Melchizedek priesthood reveal a unified narrative of God's redemptive plan. The Mosaic Covenant and the Levitical priesthood were preparatory, pointing toward the ultimate union between Christ and His Church. Under the New Covenant, this divine narrative unfolds with the Church fulfilling its dual role as Bride and priesthood, advancing the Kingdom of God while preparing for the ultimate consummation of the divine marriage covenant.

As the reborn Melchizedek priesthood, the Church embodies the divine partnership between heaven and earth. It is not merely a community of believers but an active participant in the unfolding of God's Kingdom, commissioned to intercede, proclaim, and live sacrificially. This priestly function reflects the holiness and authority of its eternal High Priest, Jesus Christ, whose perfect sacrifice established the New Covenant.

Through this covenantal framework, the Church reflects the redemptive heart of God, preserving the integrity of atonement and salvation doctrines while deepening our understanding of His eternal purpose. God's ultimate desire is to dwell in everlasting communion with a redeemed humanity—a royal priesthood and a beloved Bride.

In this divine mission, the Church is called to manifest Kingdom values and anticipate the day when the Kingdom will be fully realized. On that day, the Bridegroom and the Bride will reign together in eternal communion, fulfilling God's original design and bringing His redemptive plan to its glorious culmination.

Chapter 12: Conclusion: The Eternal Union of Covenant and Communion

Adapted Conclusion in the Manuscript's Style

As we draw this book to a close, let's reflect on the grand tapestry of God's redemptive plan—a story of love, covenant, and restoration. The journey we have undertaken has traced the intricate threads woven from the Old Covenant, a marriage between God the Father and Israel, to the New Covenant, the divine union of Jesus Christ, the Father's firstborn Son, and His Bride, the Church. These covenants are not disparate narratives but two movements of the same symphony, each revealing God's unchanging desire to dwell with humanity in eternal communion.

The Mosaic Covenant, with its statutes and rituals, was a marriage covenant, binding Israel to God in a sacred relationship. Yet, it was also a shadow of something greater—a covenant not dependent on human fidelity but sealed by the eternal faithfulness of God Himself. The New Covenant, mediated by Jesus Christ, fulfills what the Mosaic Covenant foreshadowed, inaugurating a union that transcends legalistic adherence to the Law and calls the Bride to an intimate, transformative relationship with her Bridegroom.

The Unified Narrative of Covenant and Communion

From the beginning, God's desire has been to draw humanity close, to heal the breach caused by sin, and to restore His creation to its original purpose. The Old Covenant was a preparatory stage, setting the foundation for the ultimate union. The Torah served as a divine tutor, pointing to the need for a Savior who could fulfill the Law's righteous demands and bring about the heart transformation that the Law could not accomplish.

The Church as the Reborn Melchizedek Priesthood

As we have seen, the Church is not merely a continuation of the Levitical priesthood but a rebirth of the eternal priesthood after the order of Melchizedek. This priesthood, embodied perfectly in Jesus Christ, transcends the temporal limitations of the Mosaic Covenant. It is universal, spiritual, and eternal, encompassing all who are united to Christ through faith.

In this divine narrative, the Church takes on the dual role of Bride and royal priesthood. As the Bride, the Church is called to intimacy with Christ, preparing for the ultimate consummation of the marriage covenant. As the Melchizedek priesthood, the Church intercedes for the world, proclaims the gospel, and embodies the values of the Kingdom of God. These roles are not separate but complementary, revealing the multifaceted identity of the Church as both beloved and servant, chosen and sent.

The Kingdom and the Bride

While the Church and the Kingdom of God are distinct, their missions are deeply intertwined. The Kingdom is the reign and rule of God, eternal and unshakable. The Church, as the *ekklesia* or called-out assembly, serves as the Kingdom's earthly representative, advancing its mission and reflecting its values.

In the Old Testament, the Levitical priesthood mediated between God and Israel, upholding the covenant and facilitating worship. Similarly, the Church functions as the royal priesthood of the New Covenant, mediating God's presence to the world and inviting all into His redemptive plan. This priestly role aligns with the Church's identity as the Bride, called to embody the character of her Bridegroom and prepare for the eternal reign of Christ.

The Eternal Marriage Supper

The story of the Church culminates in the Marriage Supper of the Lamb, a celebration of the eternal union between the Bridegroom and His Bride. Revelation 19:7-9 declares, "Let us rejoice and exult and give Him the glory, for the marriage of the Lamb has come, and His Bride has made herself ready." This eschatological vision is the fulfillment of every covenant, the realization of God's desire to dwell with humanity.

As the Bride of Christ, the Church anticipates this consummation, living in the tension between the already and the not-yet. Through worship, obedience, and mission, the Bride prepares for the day when the Kingdom of God will be fully realized, and every tear will be wiped away.

The Call to the Bride

The call to the Bride is not merely to await the return of the Bridegroom but to actively participate in His mission. This involves living as a royal priesthood, offering spiritual sacrifices, and proclaiming the excellencies of Him who called us out of darkness into His marvelous light (1 Peter 2:9). It also entails reflecting the love of Christ through acts of service, compassion, and justice, embodying the values of the Kingdom in a broken world.

The Bride's journey is one of sanctification and preparation, a continual process of becoming more like her Bridegroom. This is not achieved through human effort but through the transformative power of the Holy Spirit, who works within believers to produce the fruit of righteousness.

Conclusion

The Church's story, as presented in this manuscript, is one of profound beauty and divine purpose. It is the story of a Bride chosen, redeemed, and prepared for eternal union with her Bridegroom. It is the story of a royal priesthood called to intercede, proclaim, and serve as emissaries of the Kingdom of God.

As we reflect on the covenants, the priesthood, and the Kingdom, we see the hand of God weaving a tapestry of redemption that spans the ages. The Old Covenant was the foundation; the New Covenant is the fulfillment. Together, they reveal the heart of a God who longs to dwell with His people, to restore what was lost in Eden, and to bring His Bride into the joy of eternal communion.

May the Church, as the Bride of Christ and the royal priesthood in the order of Melchizedek, embrace this divine calling with faith, love, and devotion, preparing for the day when the Bridegroom will return and the Kingdom will be fully realized. In that day, the eternal song of the redeemed will echo through the heavens: "Behold, the dwelling place of God is with man" (Revelation 21:3).

| Page

Don't miss out!

Visit the website below and you can sign up to receive emails whenever Leo Gaviao publishes a new book. There's no charge and no obligation.

https://books2read.com/r/B-A-SIJAD-VJBLF

BOOKS 2 READ

Connecting independent readers to independent writers.

About the Author

Leo is a devoted follower of Christ, a passionate advocate for Christian covenant theology, and a seasoned management accountant and small business consultant. With a conviction that drives him, Leo is dedicated to making disciples of Jesus Christ and empowering others to seek the Kingdom of God.

Leo's calling to ministry is distinct, focusing on building disciples rather than planting or building churches. He firmly believes that as believers, our primary responsibility is to seek the Kingdom of God, trusting that Jesus will build His church. This conviction has led Leo to catalyze the formation of house churches in Zimbabwe and Malawi, with a significant presence in Southern Malawi.

As a gifted communicator, Leo bridges the gap between complex spiritual concepts and accessible, everyday language. His debut book, "Becoming the Bride of Christ: Mystery of the Two Covenants," delves into the rich and intricate realm of Christian covenant theology, offering readers a profound understanding of their identity and purpose in Christ.

Leo is married to Tsunagyi, and together they have four children, including one adopted girl. As a family, seeking to honor God in every aspect of their lives and see the expansion of the Kingdom of King Jesus.

Read more at leogaviao.co.zw.